Distributed Machine Learning with Python

Accelerating model training and serving with distributed systems

Guanhua Wang

BIRMINGHAM—MUMBAI

Distributed Machine Learning with Python

Copyright © 2022 Packt Publishing

Publishing Product Manager: Ali Abidi

Senior Editors: Roshan Kumar, Nathanya Diaz

Content Development Editors: Tazeen Shaikh, Shreya Moharir

Technical Editor: Devanshi Ayare

Copy Editor: Safis Editing

Project Coordinator: Aparna Ravikumar Nair

Proofreader: Safis Editing

Indexer: Pratik Shirodkar

Production Designer: Alishon Mendonca

Marketing Coordinators: Abeer Riyaz Dawe, Shifa Ansari

First published: May 2022

Production reference: 1040422

Published by Packt Publishing Ltd.

Livery Place

35 Livery Street

Birmingham

B3 2PB, UK.

ISBN 978-1-80181-569-7

www.packt.com

To my parents, Ying Han and Xin Wang

To my girlfriend, Jing Yuan

– Guanhua Wang

Contributors

About the author

Guanhua Wang is a final-year computer science Ph.D. student in the RISELab at UC Berkeley, advised by Professor Ion Stoica. His research lies primarily in the machine learning systems area, including fast collective communication, efficient in-parallel model training, and real-time model serving. His research has gained lots of attention from both academia and industry. He was invited to give talks to top-tier universities (MIT, Stanford, CMU, Princeton) and big tech companies (Facebook/Meta, Microsoft). He received his master's degree from HKUST and a bachelor's degree from Southeast University in China. He has also done some cool research on wireless networks. He likes playing soccer and has run multiple half-marathons in the Bay Area of California.

About the reviewers

Jamshaid Sohail is passionate about data science, machine learning, computer vision, and natural language processing and has more than 2 years of experience in the industry. He previously worked at a Silicon Valley-based start-up, FunnelBeam, the founders of which are from Stanford University, as a data scientist. Currently, he is working as a data scientist at Systems Limited. He has completed over 66 online courses from different platforms. He authored the book *Data Wrangling with Python 3.X* for Packt Publishing and has reviewed multiple books and courses. He is also developing a comprehensive course on data science at Educative and is in the process of writing books for multiple publishers.

Hitesh Hinduja is an ardent AI enthusiast working as a senior manager in AI at Ola Electric, where he leads a team of 20+ people in the areas of ML, statistics, CV, NLP, and reinforcement learning. He has filed 14+ patents in India and the US and has numerous research publications to his name. Hitesh has been involved in research roles at India's top business schools: the Indian School of Business, Hyderabad, and the Indian Institute of Management, Ahmedabad. He is also actively involved in training and mentoring and has been invited to be a guest speaker by various corporations and associations across the globe.

Table of Contents

3

Building a Data Parallel Training and Serving Pipeline

4

Bottlenecks and Solutions

Section 2 – Model Parallelism

5
Splitting the Model

6
Pipeline Input and Layer Split

7
Implementing Model Parallel Training and Serving Workflows

8
Achieving Higher Throughput and Lower Latency

Section 3 – Advanced Parallelism Paradigms

9
A Hybrid of Data and Model Parallelism

12

Advanced Techniques for Further Speed-Ups

Preface

Reducing time costs in machine learning leads to a shorter waiting time for model training and a faster model updating cycle. Distributed machine learning enables machine learning practitioners to shorten model training and inference time by orders of magnitude. With the help of this practical guide, you'll be able to put your Python development knowledge to work to get up and running with the implementation of distributed machine learning, including multi-node machine learning systems, in no time.

You'll begin by exploring how distributed systems work in the machine learning area and how distributed machine learning is applied to state-of-the-art deep learning models. As you advance, you'll see how to use distributed systems to enhance machine learning model training and serving speed. You'll also get to grips with applying data parallel and model parallel approaches before optimizing the in-parallel model training and serving pipeline in local clusters or cloud environments.

By the end of this book, you'll have gained the knowledge and skills needed to build and deploy an efficient data processing pipeline for machine learning model training and inference in a distributed manner.

Who this book is for

This book is for data scientists, machine learning engineers, and machine learning practitioners in both academia and industry. A fundamental understanding of machine learning concepts and working knowledge of Python programming is assumed. Prior experience implementing machine learning/deep learning models with TensorFlow or PyTorch will be beneficial. You'll find this book useful if you are interested in using distributed systems to boost machine learning model training and serving speed.

What this book covers

Chapter 1, Splitting Input Data, shows how to distribute machine learning training or serving workload on the input data dimension, which is called data parallelism.

Chapter 2, Parameter Server and All-Reduce, describes two widely-adopted model synchronization schemes in the data parallel training process.

Chapter 3, Building a Data Parallel Training and Serving Pipeline, illustrates how to implement data parallel training and the serving workflow.

Chapter 4, Bottlenecks and Solutions, describes how to improve data parallelism performance with some advanced techniques, such as more efficient communication protocols, reducing the memory footprint.

Chapter 5, Splitting the Model, introduces the vanilla model parallel approach in general.

Chapter 6, Pipeline Input and Layer Split, shows how to improve system efficiency with pipeline parallelism.

Chapter 7, Implementing Model Parallel Training and Serving Workflows, discusses how to implement model parallel training and serving in detail.

Chapter 8, Achieving Higher Throughput and Lower Latency, covers advanced schemes to reduce computation and memory consumption in model parallelism.

Chapter 9, A Hybrid of Data and Model Parallelism, combines data and model parallelism together as an advanced in-parallel model training/serving scheme.

Chapter 10, Federated Learning and Edge Devices, talks about federated learning and how edge devices are involved in this process.

Chapter 11, Elastic Model Training and Serving, describes a more efficient scheme that can change the number of accelerators used on the fly.

Chapter 12, Advanced Techniques for Further Speed-Ups, summarizes several useful tools, such as a performance debugging tool, job multiplexing, and heterogeneous model training.

To get the most out of this book

You will need to install PyTorch/TensorFlow successfully on your system. For distributed workloads, we suggest you at least have four GPUs in hand.

Software/hardware covered in the book	Domain knowledge requirements
PyTorch	Machine learning concepts (for example, loss functions and bias-variance trade-off)
TensorFlow	Deep learning concepts (forward propagation and backward propagation)
Python	Deep learning models (CNNs, RL, RNNs, and Transformers)
CUDA/C	
NVprofiler/Nsight	
Linux	

We assume you have Linux/Ubuntu as your operating system. We assume you use NVIDIA GPUs and have installed the proper NVIDIA driver as well. We also assume you have basic knowledge about machine learning in general and are familiar with popular deep learning models.

If you are using the digital version of this book, we advise you to type the code yourself or access the code from the book's GitHub repository (a link is available in the next section). Doing so will help you avoid any potential errors related to the copying and pasting of code.

Download the example code files

You can download the example code files for this book from GitHub at `https://github.com/PacktPublishing/Distributed-Machine-Learning-with-Python`. If there's an update to the code, it will be updated in the GitHub repository.

We also have other code bundles from our rich catalog of books and videos available at `https://github.com/PacktPublishing/`. Check them out!

Download the color images

We also provide a PDF file that has color images of the screenshots and diagrams used in this book. You can download it here: `https://static.packt-cdn.com/downloads/9781801815697_ColorImages.pdf`

Conventions used

There are a number of text conventions used throughout this book.

`Code in text`: Indicates code words in text, database table names, folder names, filenames, file extensions, pathnames, dummy URLs, user input, and Twitter handles. Here is an example: "Replace `YOUR_API_KEY_HERE` with the subscription key of your Cognitive Services resource. Leave the quotation marks!"

A block of code is set as follows:

```
# Connect to API through subscription key and endpoint
subscription_key = "<your-subscription-key>"
endpoint = "https://<your-cognitive-service>.cognitiveservices.azure.com/"

# Authenticate
credential = AzureKeyCredential(subscription_key)
cog_client = TextAnalyticsClient(endpoint=endpoint,
credential=credential)
```

Bold: Indicates a new term, an important word, or words that you see onscreen. For instance, words in menus or dialog boxes appear in **bold**. Here is an example: "Select **Review + Create**."

> **Tips or Important Notes**
> Appear like this.

Get in touch

Feedback from our readers is always welcome.

General feedback: If you have questions about any aspect of this book, email us at `customercare@packtpub.com` and mention the book title in the subject of your message.

Errata: Although we have taken every care to ensure the accuracy of our content, mistakes do happen. If you have found a mistake in this book, we would be grateful if you would report this to us. Please visit `www.packtpub.com/support/errata` and fill in the form.

Piracy: If you come across any illegal copies of our works in any form on the internet, we would be grateful if you would provide us with the location address or website name. Please contact us at copyright@packt.com with a link to the material.

If you are interested in becoming an author: If there is a topic that you have expertise in and you are interested in either writing or contributing to a book, please visit authors.packtpub.com.

Share Your Thoughts

Once you've read *Distributed Machine Learning with Python*, we'd love to hear your thoughts! Scan the QR code below to go straight to the Amazon review page for this book and share your feedback.

https://packt.link/r/1-801-81569-0

Your review is important to us and the tech community and will help us make sure we're delivering excellent quality content.

Section 1 – Data Parallelism

In this section, you will understand why data parallelism is needed and how it works. You will implement data-parallel training and serving pipelines and learn advanced techniques for further speed-ups.

This section comprises the following chapters:

- *Chapter 1, Splitting Input Data*
- *Chapter 2, Parameter Server and All-Reduce*
- *Chapter 3, Building a Data Parallel Training and Serving Pipeline*
- *Chapter 4, Bottlenecks and Solutions*

1
Splitting Input Data

Over the recent years, data has grown drastically in size. For instance, if you take the computer vision domain as an example, datasets such as MNIST and CIFAR-10/100 consist of only 50k training images each, whereas recent datasets such as ImageNet-1k contain over 1 million training images. However, having a larger input data size leads to a much longer model training time on a single GPU/node. In the example mentioned previously, the total training time of a useable state-of-the-art single GPU training model on a CIFAR-10/100 dataset only takes a couple of hours. However, when it comes to the ImageNet-1K dataset, the training time for a GPU model will take days or even weeks.

The standard practice for speeding up the model training process is parallel execution, which is the main focus of this book. The most popular in-parallel model training is called **data parallelism**. In data parallel training, each GPU/node holds the full copy of a model. Then, it partitions the input data into disjoint subsets, where each GPU/node is only responsible for model training on one of the input partitions. Since each GPU only trains its local model on a subset (not the whole set) of the input data, we need to conduct a procedure called model synchronization periodically. **Model synchronization** is done to ensure that, after each training iteration, all the GPUs involved in this training job are on the same page. This guarantees that the model copies that are held on different GPUs have the same parameter values.

Data parallelism can also be applied at the model serving stage. Given that the fully-trained model may need to serve a large number of inference tasks, splitting the inference input data can reduce the end-to-end model serving time as well. One major difference compared to data parallel training is that in data parallel inference, all the GPUs/nodes involved in a single job *do not* need to communicate anymore, which means that the model synchronization phase during data parallel training is completely removed.

This chapter will discuss the bottleneck of model training with large datasets and how data parallelism mitigates this.

The following topics will be covered in this chapter:

- Single-node training is too slow
- Data parallelism – the high-level bits
- Hyperparameter tuning

Single-node training is too slow

The vanilla model training process is to load both the training data and ML model into the same accelerator (for example, a GPU), which is called single-node training. There are mainly three steps that occur in a single node training model:

1. Input pre-processing
2. Training
3. Validation

The following diagram shows what this looks like in a typical model training workflow:

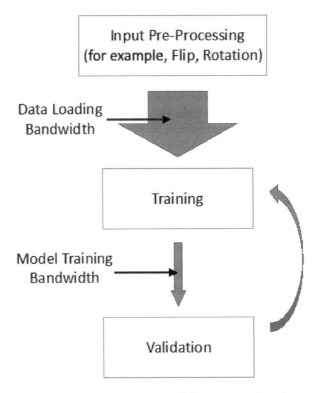

Figure 1.1 – Model training workflow on a single node

As you can see, after input pre-processing, the augmented input data is loaded into the memory of the accelerators (such as GPUs). Following that, the model is trained on the loaded input data batch and validates our trained model iteratively. The goal of this section is to discuss why single-node training is way too slow. First, we will show the real bottleneck in single-node training and then describe how data parallelism mitigates this bottleneck.

The mismatch between data loading bandwidth and model training bandwidth

Now, let's focus on the two kinds of **bandwidth (BW)** in this data pipeline, namely **data loading bandwidth** and **model training bandwidth**, as shown in the preceding diagram. Nowadays, we have more and more input data. Hence, we would ideally want the *data loading bandwidth* to be as large as possible (the wide gray arrow in the preceding diagram). However, due to the limited on-device memory of the GPUs or other accelerators, the real *model training bandwidth* is also limited (the narrow gray arrow in the preceding diagram).

Although it is generally believed that the larger input data size leads to a longer training time in single-node training, this is not true from the data flow perspective. From a system perspective, the mismatch between data loading bandwidth and model training bandwidth is the real issue. *If we can match data loading bandwidth and model training bandwidth in single-node training, it is unnecessary to conduct in-parallel model training since distributed data processing will always introduce control overheads.*

Real Bottleneck

A large input data size is not the fundamental cause of long training times in terms of single nodes. The mismatch between *data loading bandwidth* and *model training bandwidth* is the key issue.

Now that we know the reason behind the delay in single-node training when faced with large input data, let's move on to the next subtopic. Next, we will quantitively show the training times of some classic deep learning models by using standard datasets. This should help you understand why data parallel training is a must-have to deal with the mismatch between data loading bandwidth and model training bandwidth.

Single-node training time on popular datasets

Let's directly jump into training time analysis using a single GPU. We will use an NVIDIA Tesla M60 GPU as the accelerator. First, we will train both VGG-19 and ResNet-164 on the CIFAR-10 and CIFAR-100 datasets. The following diagram shows the corresponding total training time for reaching a model test accuracy over 91%:

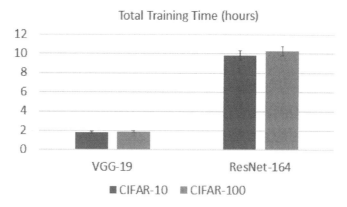

Figure 1.2 – Model training time of a single node on the CIFAR-10/100 datasets

As we can see, the total training time of VGG-19 is around 2 hours for both the CIFAR-10 and CIFAR-100 datasets, while for ResNet-164, the total training time for both the CIFAR-10 and CIFAR-100 datasets is around 10 hours.

It seems that the standard model training time, when using a single GPU on the CIFAR-10/100 dataset, is neither short nor long, which is acceptable. This is mainly because of low image resolution. For the CIFAR-10/100 datasets, the resolution of each image is very low at 32x32. Thus, the intermediate results that are generated during the model training stage are relatively small, since the activation matrices in the intermediate results are always less than 32x32. Since we generate smaller activations during training in a given fixed hardware memory size, we can train more input images at once. Consequently, we can achieve a higher *model training bandwidth*, which mitigates the mismatch between *data loading bandwidth* and *model training bandwidth*.

Now, let's look at a modern ML model training dataset, such as ImageNet-1K. We have maintained a similar training environment setup to what we had for our CIFAR-10/100 training jobs. The difference is that we are training the VGG-19 and ResNet-50 models. The following diagram shows the corresponding total training time with a single GPU setting:

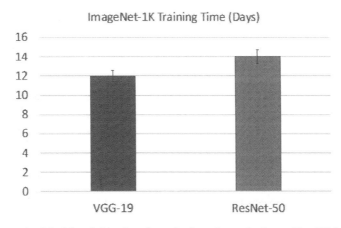

Figure 1.3 – Model training time for a single node on the ImageNet-1K dataset

As we can see, the training time on a single GPU is unacceptable. It takes around *2 weeks* to train a single model, such as VGG-19 or ResNet-50. The main reason for this much slower training speed on the ImageNet-1K dataset is the higher image resolution, which is now around 256x256. Having a higher image resolution means that each training image will have a bigger memory footprint for storing its activations, which means that we can only train a smaller amount of images at once. Thus, the gap between model training bandwidth and data loading bandwidth is larger. Furthermore, the training time can be even longer for wider and deeper model training.

For our machine learning practitioners, the whole model updating cycle is way too long if we only limit ourselves to using a single GPU. This long training time is amplified since we need to try multiple sets of hyperparameters and find the best training recipes.

Therefore, we need to adopt the data parallel training paradigm to mitigate this mismatch between data loading bandwidth and model training bandwidth.

Accelerating the training process with data parallelism

So far, we have discussed why data parallel training is a must-have due to the mismatch between *data loading bandwidth* and *model training bandwidth*. Before we dive into the details of how data parallel training works, let's look at the speed-ups that data parallelism can achieve over single node training.

Let's take ResNet-50 training on the ImageNet-1K dataset as an example. By using a proper hyperparameter setup, the following diagram shows the normalized speedups over different GPU training baselines:

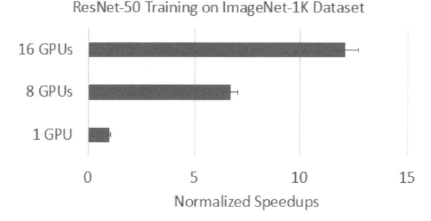

Figure 1.4 – Normalized speedups over a single GPU baseline

As we can see, we have tested the system throughput for the data parallel training process over a single GPU training baseline. By incorporating multiple GPUs into the same training job, we expanded our model training bandwidth significantly with parallelism. Ideally, the extended model training bandwidth should be linearly increased by the number of GPUs involved. Due to system control overheads and network communications introduced in data parallel training, we cannot achieve linear scaling perfectly.

However, even with system overhead involved in data parallel training, the speed-up numbers are still significant compared to a single GPU training baseline. As depicted in the preceding diagram, by incorporating 8 GPUs for data parallel training, we can increase training throughput by more than 6x. With 16 GPUs involved in the same data parallel training job, the speed-up number is even better as it can achieve near 12x higher throughput compared to the single GPU baseline. Let's convert these throughput speed-up numbers into training time: if data parallel training using 16 GPUs, we can reduce ResNet-50 training on the ImageNet-1K dataset from 14 days to around just 1-2 days.

In addition, this speed-up number can continue growing when we have more GPUs involved in the same data parallel training job. With state-of-the-art hardware such as NVIDIA's DGX-1 and DGX-2 machines, the training time of ResNet-50 on the ImageNet-1K dataset can be significantly reduced to *less than 1 hour* if we incorporate hundreds of GPUs into this data parallel model training job.

To conclude this section, single-node model training takes up a lot of time, which is mainly due to the mismatch problem between the data loading bandwidth and the model training bandwidth. By incorporating data parallelism, we can increase the model training bandwidth proportionally to the number of accelerators involved in the same training job.

Data parallelism – the high-level bits

So far, we have discussed the benefits of using data parallelism in machine learning model training, which can tremendously reduce the overall model training time. Now, we need to dive into some fundamental theories about how data parallel training works, such as **stochastic gradient descent** (**SGD**) and model synchronization. But before that, let's take a look at the system architecture for data parallel training, and how it is different from single-node training.

The simplified workflow for data parallel training is depicted in the following diagram. We have omitted some technical details during the training phase as we are mainly concerned with the two bandwidths (that is, the *data loading bandwidth* and the *model training bandwidth*):

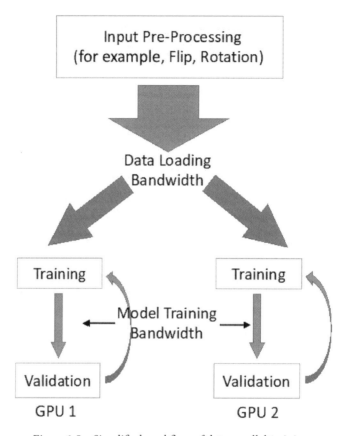

Figure 1.5 – Simplified workflow of data parallel training

As we can see, the main difference between single-node training and data parallel training is that we split the *data loading bandwidth* between multiple workers/GPUs (shown as blue arrows in the preceding diagram). Therefore, for each GPU involved in the data parallel training job, the difference between its local *data loading bandwidth* and *model training bandwidth* is much smaller compared to the single-node case.

At a high level, even though we cannot increase the *model training bandwidth* on each accelerator due to hardware limitations, we can split and balance the whole *data loading bandwidth* across multiple accelerators. And this *data loading bandwidth* split is not only applicable to data parallel training. It can be directly adopted in the data parallel model serving stage.

> **Note**
> By decreasing the per-GPU *data loading bandwidth*, data parallel training mitigates the gap between *data loading bandwidth* and *model training bandwidth* on each GPU.

At this point, we should understand how data parallel training increases end-to-end throughput by splitting the *data loading bandwidth* across multiple accelerators. After each GPU receives its local batch of augmented input data, it will conduct local model training and validation. Here, model validation in data parallel training is the same as in the single-node case (there are some small variations, which we will discuss later) and we mainly focus on the difference at the **training** stage (excluding validation).

As shown in the following diagram, in the case of a single node, we divide the model training stage into three steps: data loading, training, and model updating. As we mentioned in the *Single-node training is too slow* section, data loading is for loading new mini-batches of training data. Training is done to conduct forward and backward propagations through the model. Once we've generated gradients during backward propagation, we perform the third step; that is, updating the model parameters:

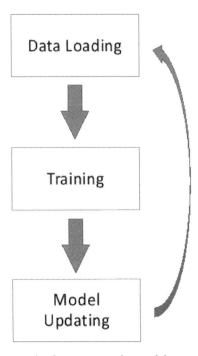

Figure 1.6 – The three steps in the model training stage

Compared to the data parallel training stage, as shown in the following diagram, there are several major differences:

- First, in data parallel training, different accelerators are trained on different batches of input data (for example, Partition 1 and Partition 2 in the following diagram). Consequently, none of the GPUs can see the full training data. Thus, traditional gradient descent optimization cannot be applied here. We also need to do a stochastic approximation of gradient descent, which can be used in the single-node case. One popular stochastic approximation method is SGD. We will look at this in more detail in the next section.

- Second, in data parallel training, besides the three steps included in single-node training, as shown in the preceding diagram, we have an additional step here called **model synchronization**, which is shown in the following diagram. Model synchronization is about collecting and aggregating local gradients that have been generated by different nodes. We will learn more about model synchronization later in this book:

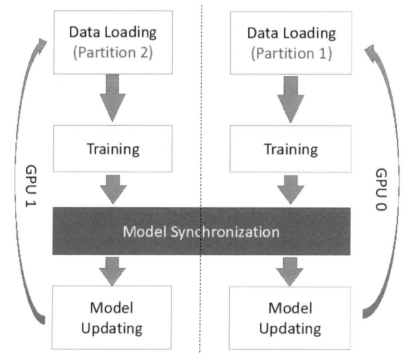

Figure 1.7 – Data parallelism procedures within the model training stage

In the next two sections, we will discuss the theoretical details about SGD and model synchronization.

Stochastic gradient descent

In this section, we will discuss why SGD is a must-have for data parallel training and how it works.

In theory, we can use traditional **gradient descent (GD)** for single-node training. It works as follows:

```
for i in dataset:
    g_all += g_i
w = w - a*g_all
```

First, we need to calculate the gradients from each data point of our training dataset, where `g_i` is the gradients. Here, we calculate this on the `i`-th training data point. The formal definition of `g_i` is as follows:

$$g\_i = \frac{dL(w)_i}{dw}$$

Then, we sum up all the gradients that have been calculated by all the training data points (`g_all += g_i`) and then do a single step model update with `w = w - a*g_all`.

However, in data parallel training, each GPU can only see part of (not the full) training dataset, which makes it impossible to use traditional GD optimization since we cannot calculate `g_all` in this case. Thus, SGD is a must-have. In addition, SGD is also applicable to single-node training. SGD works as follows:

```
for i in dataset:
    w = w - a*g_i
```

Basically, instead of updating the model weights (*w*) after generating the gradients from *all* the training data, SGD allows for model weights updates using *a single or a few training samples* (for example, a mini-batch). With this relaxation of model updating restrictions, the workers in data parallel training can update their model weights using their local (not global) training samples.

> **GD versus SGD**
>
> In GD, we need to compute the gradients over *all* the training data and update the model weights.
>
> In SGD, we compute the gradients over a *subset* of all the training data and update the model weights.

However, since each worker updates their model weights based on their local training data, the model parameters of different workers can be different after each of the training iterations. Therefore, we need to conduct *model synchronization* periodically to guarantee that all the workers are on the same page, meaning that they maintain the model parameters after each training iteration.

Model synchronization

As we saw previously, in data parallel training, different workers train their local models using disjointed subsets of the total training data, so the trained model weights may be different. To force all the workers to have the same view of the model parameters, we need to conduct model synchronization.

Let's study this in a simple four-GPU setting, as shown in the following diagram:

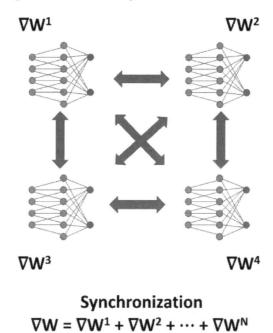

Synchronization

$$\nabla W = \nabla W^1 + \nabla W^2 + \cdots + \nabla W^N$$

Figure 1.8 – Model synchronization in a four-GPU setting

As we can see, we have four GPUs in a data parallel training job. Here, each GPU maintains a copy of the full ML model locally inside its on-device memory.

Let's assume that all the GPUs are initialized with the same model parameters, which is a standard practice, by setting the randomize function with a fixed seed.

After the first training iteration, each GPU will generate its local gradients as ∇W^i, where i refers to the i-th GPU. Given that they are training on different local training inputs, all the gradients from different GPUs may be different. To guarantee that all four GPUs have the same model updates, we need to conduct model synchronization before the model parameter updates:

$$\nabla W^i$$

Model synchronization does two things:

1. Collects and sums up all the gradients from all the GPUs in use, as shown here:

$$\nabla W = \nabla W^1 + \nabla W^2 + \nabla W^3 + \ldots + \nabla W^N$$

2. Broadcasts the aggregated gradients to all the GPUs.

Once the model synchronization steps have been completed, we can get the aggregated gradients, ∇W, locally on each GPU. Then, we can use these aggregated gradients, ∇W, for the model updates, which guarantees that the updated model parameters remain the same after this first data parallel training iteration.

Similarly, in the following training iterations, we conduct model synchronization after each GPU generates its local gradients. So, model synchronization guarantees that the model parameters remain the same after every training iteration in a particular data parallel training job.

For the real system implementations, this model synchronization mainly has two different variations: the *parameter server architecture* and the *All-Reduce architecture*, which we will discuss in detail in the next chapter.

So far, we have come across some of the key concepts in data parallel training jobs, such as SGD and model synchronization. Next, we will discuss some important hyperparameters related to data parallel training.

Hyperparameter tuning

In this section, we will focus on the hyperparameters that are closely related to data parallel training: global batch size, learning rate adjustment, and optimizer selection.

Let's discuss them one by one.

> **Notes on Hyperparameters**
> While some of these hyperparameters have existed in the standard single-node training process, in data parallel training, these parameters may have new searching dimensions and new correlations.

Global batch size

The global batch size refers to how many training samples will be loaded into all the GPUs for training simultaneously. The counterpart of this concept in single-node training is the batch size or mini-batch.

Selecting the proper global batch size is different from selecting a single node's batch size. In single-node training, we always set the batch size to be the *maximum* number that can fit into the accelerator's memory without causing **out-of-memory** (**OOM**) issues. In data parallel training, given N GPUs, we may *not* set the global batch-size to be $N*Max(single\_node)$, where *Max(single_node)* refers to the maximum batch size on a single GPU.

In data parallel training, this global batch size is the first hyperparameter we need to search or fine-tune. If the global batch size is too large, the training model may not converge. If the global batch size is too small, it is just a waste of distributed computational resources.

Learning rate adjustment

Since we have used a very large global batch size compared to single node training, we also need to adjust the learning rate accordingly.

> **Rule of Thumb Regarding Learning Rate Adjustment**
> The rule of thumb policy for determining the learning rate in data parallel training is to multiply the learning rate in the single-node case by N, if we use N GPUs to do the data parallel training together.

Recent research literature suggests that, for large-batch data parallel training, we should have a warmup stage at the very beginning of the training stage. This warmup policy suggests that we should start data parallel training with a relatively small learning rate. After this warmup period, we should gradually increase the learning rate for several epochs of training, and then stop increasing the learning rate by defining a peak learning rate.

Model synchronization schemes

Now that we have chosen our optimizer (global batch size) and adjusted the learning rate accordingly, the next thing we need to do is select an appropriate model synchronization model to use. We need this because we need to initialize a group of processes to run our data parallel training job in a distributed manner, where each process will be responsible for handling model synchronization on one machine or one GPU.

Let's take `pytorch` as an example. Here, you need to initialize your process groups, as follows:

```
torch.distributed.init_process_group(backend='nccl',
                                     init_method = '...',
                                     world_size = N,
                                     timeout = M)
```

Here, the first parameter (`backend='nccl'`) we need to choose from is the model synchronization backend. Right now, deep learning platforms such as PyTorch mainly support three different communication backends: NCCL, Gloo, and MPI.

The main differences among these three communication backends are as follows:

- **NCCL**:

  - GPU only

  - No support for one-to-all communication primitives such as Scatter   *has broadcast*

  - No support for all-to-one communication primitives such as Gather   *has reduce*

- **Gloo**:

  - Mainly support for CPU, partial support for GPU.

  - For CPU, it supports most communication primitives.

  - For GPU, it only supports the most commonly used communication primitives, such as Broadcast and All-Reduce.

  - No support for all-to-all communication.

- **MPI**:

  - CPU only

  - Supports special hardware communication, such as IP over InfiniBand

Among these three, the following are some high-level suggestions on selecting communication schemes:

- For GPU clusters, use NCCL.
- For CPU clusters, use Gloo first. If that doesn't work, try MPI.

With that, we have discussed three main communication schemes we can use in data parallel training jobs. Since the nodes we have used for model training are GPUs, we usually set NCCL as our default communication backend.

Summary

After reading this chapter, you should be able to explore and find the real bottleneck in single-node training. You should also know how data parallelism mitigates this bottleneck in single-node training, thus increasing the overall throughput. Finally, you should know about the several main hyperparameters related to data parallel training.

In the next chapter, we will focus on two major system architectures for data parallel training, namely the **parameter server** (**PS**) and **All-Reduce** paradigms.

2
Parameter Server and All-Reduce

As described in *Chapter 1*, *Splitting Input Data*, to keep model consistency among all the GPUs/nodes involved in a data parallel training job, we need to conduct model synchronization. In terms of this model synchronization core, distributed system architectures for data parallel training must be built up.

To guarantee model consistency, two methodologies can be applied.

First, we can keep the model parameters in one place (a centralized node). Whenever a GPU/node needs to conduct model training, it pulls the parameters from the centralized node, trains the model, then pushes back model updates to the centralized node. Model consistency is guaranteed since all the GPUs/nodes are pulling from the same centralized node. This is what is called the **parameter server** paradigm.

Second, every GPU/node keeps a copy of the model parameters so we force the model copies to synchronize periodically. Each GPU trains its local model replica using its own training data partition. After each training iteration, the model replicas that are held on different GPUs can be different since they are trained with different input data. Therefore, we inject a global synchronization step after each training iteration. This averages the parameters that are held on different GPUs so that model consistency can be guaranteed in this fully distributed manner. This is known as the **All-Reduce** paradigm.

The main goal of this chapter is to discuss and compare the two main data parallel training paradigms, namely parameter server and All-Reduce. After going through this chapter, you will know how to design a data parallel training pipeline with both the parameter server and All-Reduce paradigms.

First, we will describe the system architecture of the parameter server paradigm. Then, we will discuss how to implement the parameter server architecture using **PyTorch**. Following that, we will highlight some of the shortcomings of parameter server and the reasons why people tend to replace parameter server with All-Reduce. After that, we will describe the more recent All-Reduce paradigm for data parallel training. We will end this chapter by talking about the broader family of collective communication, which includes All-Reduce.

The chapter will cover the following topics:

- Parameter server architecture
- Implementing the parameter server
- Issues with the parameter server
- All-Reduce architecture
- Collective communication

Technical requirements

The library dependencies for running the code in this chapter are as follows:

- `torch>=1.8.1`
- `torchvision>=0.9.1`
- `cuda>=11.0`
- `NVIDIA driver >=450.119.03`

Installing these GPU drivers and PyTorch libraries is mandatory. We suggest that you install the latest versions for the best performance.

Parameter server architecture

In this section, we will dive into the system architecture of the parameter server paradigm. The domain knowledge requirements for this section are as follows:

- A Master/Worker architecture in distributed systems

- Client/Server communication

The **parameter server architecture** mainly consists of two roles: **parameter server** and **worker**. The parameter server can be regarded as the master node in the traditional Master/Worker architecture.

Workers are the computer nodes or GPUs that are responsible for model training. We split the total training data among all the workers. Each worker trains their local model with the training data partition that's been assigned to it.

The duties of parameter server are twofold:

- Aggregate model updates from all the workers.

- Update the model parameters held on the parameter server.

The following diagram depicts a simplified parameter server architecture with two workers and one parameter server in the system:

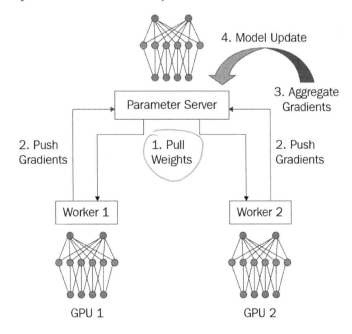

Figure 2.1 – The parameter server architecture with a single server node

The whole system works through the following four stages:

1. **Pull Weights**: All the workers pull the model parameters/weights from the centralized parameter server.

2. **Push Gradients**: Each worker trains its local model with its local training data partition and generates local gradients. Then, all the workers push their local gradients to the centralized parameter server.

3. **Aggregate Gradients**: After collecting all the gradients that have been sent from the worker nodes, the parameter server will sum up all the gradients.

4. **Model Update**: Once the aggregated gradients have been calculated, the parameter server uses the aggregated gradients to update the model parameters on this centralized server.

As we can see, for each training iteration, we conduct these four steps among the parameter server and workers. We loop over these four steps for the whole model training process. However, the communication in the parameter server architecture can often be the training bottleneck.

Communication bottleneck in the parameter server architecture

As shown in the preceding diagram, on the communication side, there are mainly two types of communication – **Pull Weights** and **Push Gradients**:

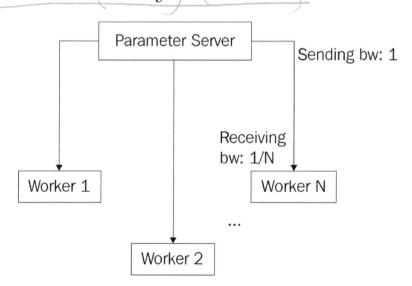

Figure 2.2 – Fan-out communication for pulling weights

First, let's look at the communication pattern of pulling the weights from the parameter server to all the workers. As shown in the preceding diagram, this is a one-to-all communication where the centralized parameter server needs to send out model weights simultaneously to all the worker nodes. This is called a **fan-out** communication pattern.

Now, let's assume that the communication bandwidth of each node (for both the parameter server and workers) is *1*. Let's also assume that we have *N* workers in this data parallel training job.

Since the centralized parameter server needs to send the model to *N* workers concurrently, the sending **bandwidth** (**BW**) to each worker is only *1/N*. On the other hand, the receiving bandwidth for each worker is 1, which is much larger than the parameter server's sending bandwidth of *1/N*. Therefore, during the pulling weights stage, we have a communication bottleneck on the parameter server side.

> **Fan-Out Weights Pulling**
>
> For an *N* workers and *1* parameter server setting, the worker receiving bandwidth (*1*) is much higher than the parameter server sending bandwidth (*1/N*). Therefore, the communication bottleneck is on the parameter server's side while pulling the weights.

Now, let's look at the communication pattern during the gradient pushing process. As shown in the following diagram, during this process, all the GPUs concurrently send their local gradients to the centralized parameter server. This is called a **fan-in** communication pattern:

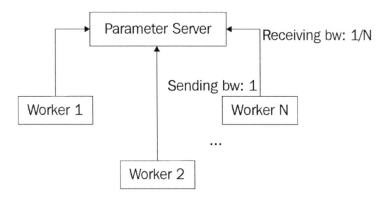

Figure 2.3 – Fan-in communication for pushing gradients

We still assume all the nodes (both the parameter server and workers) have the same network bandwidth of *1*. Given *N* workers in the parameter server architecture, each worker can send its local gradients with a sending bandwidth of *1*.

However, since the parameter server needs to receive gradients from all the workers at the same time, the receiving bandwidth for each worker is just *1/N*. Therefore, the communication bottleneck is still on the parameter server's side during the pushing gradients stage.

> **Fan-In Gradients Pushing**
>
> For an *N* workers and *1* parameter server setting, the worker sending bandwidth (*1*) is much higher than the parameter server receiving bandwidth (*1/N*). Therefore, the communication bottleneck is on the parameter server's side during gradients pushing.

Sharding the model among parameter servers

As we mentioned previously, the communication bottleneck is always on the centralized parameter server side. We can solve this issue via load balancing.

With the same example provided in the previous sections, we have *N* workers, and each node has a communication bandwidth of *1*. Instead of having one *parameter server*, we split the model into *N* parameter servers, where each server is responsible for updating the model of *1/N* model parameters:

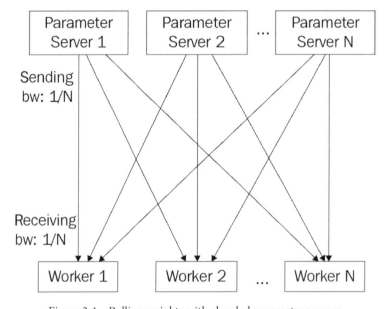

Figure 2.4 – Pulling weights with sharded parameter servers

As shown in the preceding diagram, given that we have N parameter servers, now, each worker can concurrently pull the model parameters from all N parameter servers. For each worker, it receives data from each parameter server with a bandwidth of $1/N$. Thus, for each worker, the total amount of receiving bandwidth from all the parameter servers is $1/N * N = 1$, which fully saturates the link bandwidth of this worker node. The communication bottleneck is removed since all the workers can receive data at its maximum bandwidth:

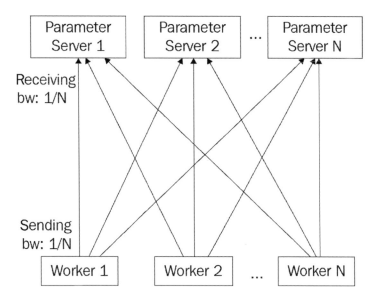

Figure 2.5 – Pushing gradients with sharded parameter servers

As we can see, during the pushing gradients stage, each worker can send gradients to all the parameter servers concurrently with a bandwidth of $1/N$ each. The communication bottleneck on the parameter servers has been removed since all the workers can transmit data at their maximum bandwidth.

It is worth mentioning that the number of workers and parameter servers don't necessarily have to be equivalent. Having a sharded model among multiple parameter servers always mitigates the network bottlenecks on the parameter server side. In practice, the number of parameter servers should be no more than the number of workers.

In this section, we discussed the system architecture of the parameter server. In the next section, we illustrate how to implement it in detail.

Implementing the parameter server

Previously, we discussed the parameter server architecture and its variations. Now, let's dive into the implementation of the data pipeline for the parameter server architecture. The technical requirements for this section are as follows:

- The PyTorch and TorchVision libraries
- The MNIST dataset

For the environment setup, we have used CUDA 11.0 and PyTorch 3.7. We have trained a simple **convolution neural network** (**CNN**) on the MNIST dataset. First, we must define our model structure. Then, we will highlight the key functions of the parameter server and workers.

Defining model layers

First, we will define a simple CNN model, as shown in the following snippet:

```
class MyNet(nn.Module):
  def __init__(self):
    ...
  def forward(self, x):
    x = self.conv1(x)
    x = self.dropout1(x)
    x = F.relu(x)
    x = self.conv2(x)
    x = self.dropout2(x)
    x = F.max_pool2d(x,2)
    x = torch.flatten(x,1)
    x = self.fc1(x)
    x = F.relu(x)
    x = self.fc2(x)
    x = F.relu(x)
    x = self.fc3(x)
    output = F.log_softmax(x, dim = 1)
    return output
```

For MNIST dataset training, we must define a simple CNN with five key function layers: two convolution layers, followed by three **fully connected (FC)** layers. Among these key function layers, we must inject dropout/pooling and ReLU layers in-between to increase the model's non-linearity and robustness.

Note that the model can be initialized in any device, such as a CPU or GPU, plus many others. This means that we can initialize the same model structure for both the parameter server and workers. Furthermore, for the parameter server, we can easily split the model into multiple GPUs by setting different layers for different devices.

Defining the parameter server

In the parameter server, we need to initialize two things: a model and an optimizer. As illustrated in the following snippet, the optimizer we are using is **stochastic gradient descent (SGD)**, which we discussed in *Chapter 1, Splitting Input Data*:

```
class ParameterServer(nn.Module):
  def __init__(self):
    super().__init__()
    self.model = MyNet()
    ...
    self.optimizer = optim.SGD(self.model.parameters(), lr =
0.05)
```

Next, we need to define two key functions:

```
def get_weights(self):
  return self.model.state_dict()
```

The first one is the get_weights() function, which is used to get up-to-date model parameters. It is defined as follows. Here, we call the internal PyTorch function to pull out model parameters.

The second function is to update the model with the gradients that have been generated from the workers, which is called the update_model() function. After receiving the gradients that have been generated by the worker nodes, we can use this function to update the parameter values of the model on the parameter server.

The `update_model()` function is defined as follows:

```
def update_model(self, grads):
    for para, grad in zip(self.model.parameters(), grads):
        para.grad = grad
    self.optimizer.step()
    self.optimizer.zero_grad()
```

After receiving the gradients of the whole model, we iterate both the model parameters and gradients over the model layers. For each layer weight (`para`), we assign its gradients accordingly.

Once we've done this, we use a predefined SGD optimizer to update the model parameter values on the parameter server. Then, we zero out the gradients and wait for the next training iteration.

Defining the worker

Previously, we illustrated how to implement the parameter server class object. Now, let's define our `Worker` class object:

```
class Worker(nn.Module):
    def __init__(self):
        super().__init__()
        self.model = MyNet()
        if torch.cuda.is_available():
            self.input_device = torch.device("cuda:0")
        else:
            self.input_device = torch.device("cpu")
```

First, we need to define the initialization function of `Worker()`. With the preceding initialization, we can easily switch the `Worker()` object so that it runs on multiple devices by initializing `MyNet()` and assigning `Worker.input_device` to different `GPU_ids` (example: `cuda:1`).

Similar to the parameter server, we also have two key functions in the `Worker()` object, namely `pull_weights()` and `push_gradients()`.

The `pull_weights()` function is used to get the model parameter values from the parameter server. It is defined as follows:

```
def pull_weights(self, model_params):
    self.model.load_state_dict(model_params)
```

This loads the model weights from the parameter server to its local model replica.

The `push_gradients()` function is used for model training and generating gradients. It is defined as follows:

```
def push_gradients(self, batch_idx, data, target):
    data, target = data.to(self.input_device),
                target.to(self.input_device)
    output = self.model(data)
    data.requires_grad = True
    loss = F.nll_loss(output, target)
    loss.backward()
    grads = []
    for layer in self.parameters():
        grad = layer.grad
        grads.append(grad)
    print(f"batch {batch_idx} training :: loss {loss.item()}")
    return grads
```

This function works as follows:

1. We move the training data and labels to the device that runs the `Worker()` object.
2. We set the `data.requires_grad = True` flag so that we can get the gradients that have been generated over the training data.
3. We calculate the loss and perform backward propagation to generate gradients.
4. We collect the gradients for each layer and return the aggregated gradients.

Now that we have both the `ParameterServer()` and `Worker()` objects, we will learn how these two parties communicate.

Passing data between the parameter server and worker

Before connecting the parameter server and the worker, we need to load the training data into the worker nodes. We can define `train_loader()` for this, as follows:

```
train_loader =torch.utils.data.DataLoader(\
datasets.MNIST('./mnist_data', download=True, train=True,
                transform=transforms.Compose(\
[transforms.ToTensor(),
                transforms.Normalize((0.1307,),(0.3081,))])),
                batch_size=128, shuffle=True)
```

Basically, once the data has been downloaded, this code conducts data preprocessing, as we discussed in *Chapter 1, Splitting Input Data*.

Now, we must define the `main()` function to connect the parameter server and the worker. It is defined as follows:

```
def main():
    ps = ParameterServer()
    worker = Worker()

    for batch_idx, (data, target) in enumerate(train_loader):
        params = ps.get_weights()
        worker.pull_weights(params)
        grads = worker.push_gradients(batch_idx, data, target)
        ps.update_model(grads)
```

First, we initialize both the parameter server (ps) and the worker. Then, for each form of batch training, the following occurs:

1. We pull the up-to-date weights from the parameter server.
2. We let the worker pull the weights and update its local model parameters.
3. We calculate the gradients.
4. We let the parameter server update the model weights with the gradients from *Step 3*.

We loop over these four functions for each batch training interation.

After completing these steps, we must run the main function, as follows:

```
$ python main.py
```

This will report the loss value after each training iteration, as follows:

```
batch 0 training :: loss 2.3417391777038574
batch 1 training :: loss 2.321241855621338
batch 2 training :: loss 2.324983596801758
...
batch 467 training :: loss 0.24062871932983398
batch 468 training :: loss 0.2222810834646225
Done Training
```

Now, we have a simple parameter server architecture with both a parameter server and a worker. We can easily add more workers by initializing the Worker() object on multiple GPUs. We can also split the single parameter server into shared ones by assigning different model layers to different GPUs.

Issues with the parameter server

In recent years, fewer and fewer machine learning practitioners have been using the parameter server paradigm for their data parallel training jobs. The main reason for this decrease in the popularity of the parameter server architecture is twofold.

Given N nodes, it is unclear what the best ratio is between the parameter server and workers.

As we've mentioned previously, in the *parameter server architecture*, we have two roles:

- Parameter server:

  - Never do training, 0 training BW

  - More PS, higher communication BW, less model synchronization latency

- Worker:

  - More Workers, higher training BW

  - More Workers, more data transfer, higher model synchronization overhead

We need to balance *training throughput* and *communication latency*. We will discuss this trade-off in the following two cases.

Case 1 – more parameter servers

If we assign more nodes as parameter servers, we have fewer data to communicate since we have fewer workers to synchronize. Since we have more parameter servers, we have a higher network bandwidth. This model synchronization latency can be defined as follows:

Model_sync_latency = Amount_of_data / Total_communication_bw

Thus, *more parameter servers means a lower communication latency*.

On the training throughput side, since parameter workers do not contribute to the training BW, *fewer workers mean we have a lower training throughput*.

Case 2 – more Workers

On the contrary, if we assign more nodes as Workers, we have more data to communicate since more workers need to be synchronized. Since we have fewer parameter servers, we have a lower communication bandwidth. Thus, given the preceding equation, *more workers means a higher communication latency*.

On the training throughput side, *more workers means we have a higher training throughput*.

> **The Trade-Off Between Training Throughput and Communication Latency**
>
> Given N number of nodes, it is hard to determine the best ratio between the number of parameter servers and the number of Workers.
>
> More parameter servers means lower communication latency but lower training throughput, while more Workers means higher communication latency but higher training throughput.

The parameter server architecture introduces a high coding complexity for practitioners

From our previous implementation section, we have seen that the coding complexity that's introduced by the parameter server architecture is mainly twofold:

1. We need to explicitly define the `Worker()` and `ParameterSever()` objects. We also need to implement extra functions within these objects.

2. We need to explicitly define the communication handles/pointers for both the workers and parameter servers. In addition, we also need to implement data transfer protocol repeatedly if the hardware environments change (for example, the number of parameter servers changes, the number of workers changes, the network topology among the nodes changes).

Given these two main shortcomings of the parameter server architecture, people tend to switch to another data parallel training paradigm called All-Reduce.

All-Reduce architecture

So far, we have discussed the parameter server architecture, its implementation, and its shortcomings.

Next, we will look at the All-Reduce architecture for data parallel training process.

In the **All-Reduce** architecture, we abandon the parameter server role in the parameter server architecture. Now, every node is equivalent and all of them are worker nodes.

This all-worker methodology directly addresses the two main shortcomings in the parameter server architecture:

- First, since we only have workers, given N nodes, we do not need to determine the ratio between the parameter servers and workers. We just treat all the nodes as workers.

- Second, we only need to define worker objects. Furthermore, we leave the burden of implementing communication protocols to standard collective communication libraries such as NCCL and Blink.

The All-Reduce paradigm is borrowed from the traditional **Message Passing Interface** (**MPI**) domain. Before we talk about All-Reduce, let's explore how Reduce works.

Reduce

First, let's look at a simpler collective primitive related to All-Reduce, called **Reduce**.

The following diagram shows a three-worker Reduce setting, where we conduct the Reduce operation from **Worker 1**, **Worker 2**, and **Worker 3** to **Worker 1**:

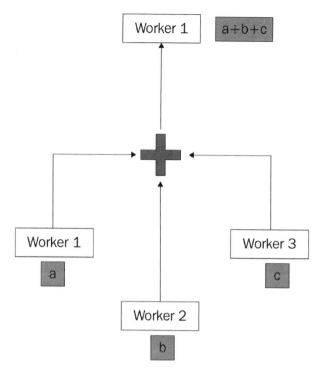

Figure 2.6 – The Reduce primitive in a three-workers setting

As we can see, the Reduce operator (that is, +) is used to aggregate the values from different nodes and store them in a single node. Some of the most common Reduce operators are as follows:

- Sum
- Averaging
- Multiplication

The most widely used Reduce operator is sum.

As shown in the preceding diagram, initially, **Worker 1** has a value of **a**, **Worker 2** has a value of **b**, and **Worker 3** has a value of **c**. Once we have used the Reduce function with the sum operator, we aggregate the values from **Worker 1**, **Worker 2**, and **Worker 3** into **Worker 1**. Therefore, after using the Reduce function on **Worker 1**, **Worker 1** maintains the value of **a+b+c** instead of **a**.

Note that after using this Reduce function, the values held on **Worker 2** and **Worker 3** do not change. More precisely, after using Reduce function, the value on **Worker 2** is still **b**, and the value on **Worker 3** is still **c**.

As shown in the preceding diagram, the communication pattern of Reduce is an all-to-one communication, which means all the nodes send their local values to the Reduce node.

All-Reduce

Before we discuss the Reduce function, let's check out the All-Reduce function. As we mentioned in the previous section, there is one node that maintains the aggregated value. All-Reduce allows all the nodes to get the same aggregated value:

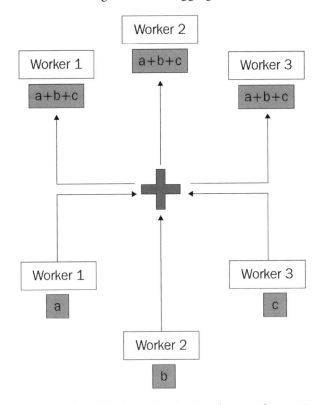

Figure 2.7 – The All-Reduce primitive in a three-workers setting

As we can see, before the All-Reduce function is used, **Worker 1** holds a value of **a**, **Worker 2** holds a value of **b**, and **Worker 3** holds a value of **c**. It is different from the Reduce function as it only allows one node to have the final aggregated value (that is, **a+b+c**); every worker will get the aggregated value once the All-Reduce operation has been performed.

Now, let's imagine that the values of workers are their gradients. The All-Reduce function allows all the workers to get the aggregated gradients from all the worker nodes. *This gradient aggregation is the model synchronization procedure in the All-Reduce architecture.* It guarantees that all the workers are using the same gradient to update the model in the current training iteration.

More precisely, the models are synchronized in the following steps:

1. In the beginning, all the workers are initialized with the same model parameter values.

2. After one training iteration, the models on the different workers are synchronized since the gradient values for model updating are the same once the All-Reduce function has been used.

3. Loop over *Step 2* until training ends.

For the communication pattern, All-Reduce extends Reduce's all-to-one communication to all-to-all communication. As shown in the preceding diagram, every worker needs to send its value to all the other workers.

Ring All-Reduce

Previously, we discussed Reduce and how it can be extended to All-Reduce. In this section, we will discuss a popular implementation of the All-Reduce function called **Ring All-Reduce**. Ring All-Reduce has been widely adopted in deep learning frameworks such as PyTorch Distributed and TensorFlow.

Several popular implementations of Ring All-Reduce are as follows:

*   NVIDIA NCCL

*   Uber Horovod

*   Facebook Gloo

Now, let's discuss how Ring All-Reduce works in real hardware environments. We will use the three-workers example for illustration purposes. Each step describes the relevant diagram:

- *Step 1*: **Worker 1** has a value of **a**, **Worker 2** has a value of **b**, and **Worker 3** has a value of **c**:

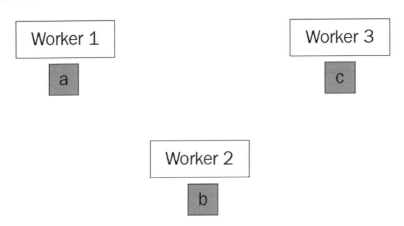

Figure 2.8 – Step 1 of Ring All-Reduce in a three-workers setting

- *Step 2*: **Worker 1** has a value of **a**. **Worker 1** passes this value, **a**, to **Worker 2**. **Worker 2** gets **a+b**. **Worker 3** still has a value of **c**:

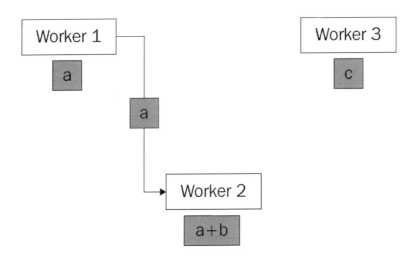

Figure 2.9 – Step 2 of Ring All-Reduce in a three-workers setting

- *Step 3*: **Worker 1** has a value of **a**. **Worker 2** has a value of **a+b**, which it passes to **Worker 3**. **Worker 3** now has a value of **a+b+c**:

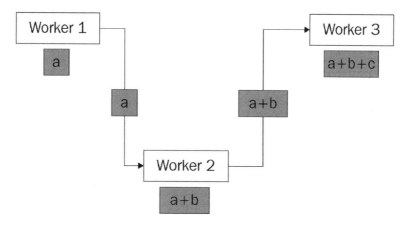

Figure 2.10 – Step 3 of Ring All-Reduce in a three-workers setting

- *Step 4*: **Worker 3** passes **a+b+c** to **Worker 1**. **Worker 1** now has **a+b+c**. **Worker 2** now has **a+b**. **Worker 3** now has **a+b+c**:

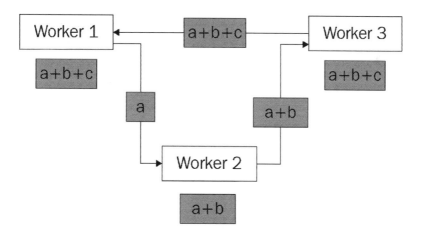

Figure 2.11 – Step 4 of Ring All-Reduce in a three-workers setting

- *Step 5*: **Worker 1**, who has **a+b+c**, passes **a+b+c** to **Worker 2**. **Worker 2** now has **a+b+c** and **Worker 3** has **a+b+c** as well:

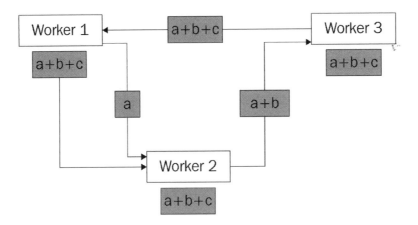

Figure 2. 12 – Step 5 of Ring All-Reduce in a three-workers setting

In this three-GPU setting, Ring All-Reduce completes after going through all these steps.

Now that we have covered all the main topics regarding performing All-Reduce for data parallel training, we will look at more related communication primitives in the next section.

Collective communication

Besides the popular All-Reduce function, collective communication has a wide family of message-passing functions. We will discuss several of the most important collective communication functions in this section, namely Broadcast, Gather, and All-Gather.

Broadcast

Broadcast is also widely used in the All-Reduce architecture. For example, we can use Broadcast to distribute the initial model weights among all the workers. The following diagram shows an example of the Broadcast function in a three-workers setting:

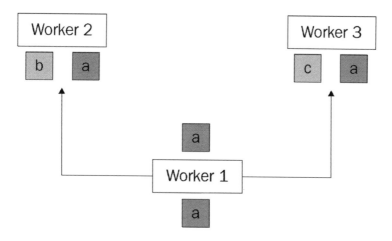

Figure 2.13 – Broadcast in a three-workers setting

As we can see, initially, **Worker 1** holds a value of **a**. **Worker 2** holds a value of **b**, while **Worker 3** holds a value of **c**. Here, we conduct a broadcast from **Worker 1** to all the other workers.

After this broadcast operation, **Worker 1** still holds a value of **a**. However, **Worker 2** now holds values **a** and **b**. On the other hand, **Worker 3** holds values **a** and **c**.

For this communication pattern, Broadcast is a one-to-all communication primitive.

Gather

Gather can be regarded as an inverse operation of Broadcast. The Gather node will collect all the values from all the other nodes simultaneously:

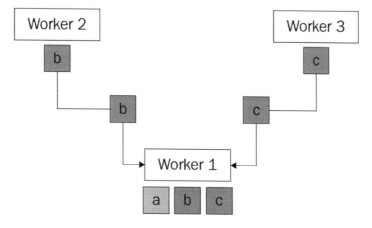

Figure 2.14 – Gather in a three workers setting

As we can see, we use the Gather function on **Worker 1**. During the Gather operation, both **Worker 2** and **Worker 3** will send their local values to **Worker 1** concurrently.

After performing the Gather function on **Worker 1**, **Worker 1** will get all the values from all the workers. However, all the other workers still maintain their initial values before this Gather function call.

For the communication pattern, Gather is an all-to-one communication primitive, which is similar to Reduce. The only difference is that Gather only collects data from all the workers. There is no reduce operation (for example, sum), similar to what the Reduce primitive has.

All-Gather

To extend Gather so that it's an all-to-all function, we can introduce the All-Gather operation.

All-Gather is a very expensive operation. Avoid using it if it's not necessary.

For each worker, it is equivalent to performing Broadcast and Gather simultaneously. For example, let's look at **Worker 1** in *Figure 2.15*.

To complete All-Gather, **Worker 1** needs to do the following:

- Broadcast its local value to **Worker 2** and **Worker 3.**
- Gather all the values from **Worker 2** and **Worker 3.**

During All-Gather, all the other workers send and receive data simultaneously, which is similar to what **Worker 1** does.

All-Gather is more expensive than All-Reduce regarding its network bandwidth usage. The main reason for this is that every worker sends/receives their raw data in All-Gather. There is no data aggregation like what we have in All-Reduce. Thus, the total amount of data transfer in All-Gather is way more than in All-Reduce:

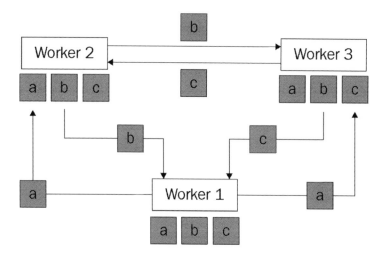

Figure 2.15 – All-Gather in a three-workers setting

With this, we have come to the end of this chapter.

Summary

In this chapter, we mainly discussed the two most popular data parallel training paradigms: parameter server and All-Reduce. You should now know about the Parameter Server architecture, its implementation, and its shortcomings. You should also understand the All-Reduce architecture and its broader family of collective communications.

In the next chapter, we will focus on implementing the whole model training and serving pipeline using data parallelism.

3

Building a Data Parallel Training and Serving Pipeline

In the previous chapter, we discussed the two main-stream data parallel training paradigms, **parameter server** and **All-Reduce**. Due to the shortcomings of the parameter server paradigm, the mainstream solution for data parallel training is the All-Reduce architecture. We will illustrate our implementation using the All-Reduce paradigm.

In this chapter, we will mainly focus on the coding side of data parallelism. Before we dive into the details, we will list the assumptions we have for the implementations in this chapter:

- We will use homogenous hardware for all our training nodes.

- All our training nodes will be exclusively used for a single job, which means no resource sharing in multi-tenant clusters.

- The number of accelerators will always be sufficient for our needs.

First, we will describe the entire training pipeline and highlight the major components, which include data preprocessing, data loading, training, model synchronization, and model updates. Following that, we will discuss the implementation in two different settings: single-machine multi-GPU and multi-machine multi-GPU. Next, we will illustrate how to checkpoint the model and its relevant metadata during training. Moving on, we will explain how to leverage massive compute nodes to conduct model evaluation and hyperparameter tuning. We will end this chapter by discussing how to implement data parallel model serving.

In this chapter, we will be covering the following main topics:

- The data parallel training pipeline in a nutshell
- Single-machine multi-GPUs and multi-machine multi-GPUs
- Checkpointing and fault tolerance
- Model evaluation and hyperparameter tuning
- Model serving in data parallelism

Technical requirements

For the implementation in this chapter, we will use a simple CNN as our model and use MNIST as our dataset. We will use PyTorch for illustration purposes. The main library dependencies for this chapter's code are as follows:

- `torch>=1.8.1`
- `torchvision>=0.9.1`
- `cuda>=11.0`
- `NVIDIA driver >=450.119.03`

It is mandatory to have the correct versions of these libraries installed before proceeding with the chapter.

The data parallel training pipeline in a nutshell

In this section, we will mainly focus on using the All-Reduce-based data parallel architecture. Here, we will wrap up the whole data parallel training pipeline. The whole training workflow is shown in the following diagram:

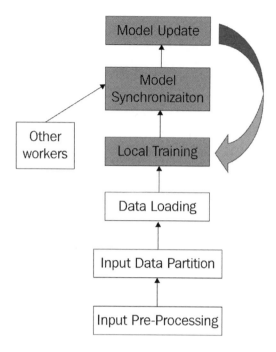

Figure 3.1 – Parameter server architecture with a single server node

As we can see, the training pipeline of each worker consists of six steps:

1. **Input Pre-Processing**: Given the raw training input data, we need to pre-process it. Common input pre-processing techniques include image crop, image flip, input data normalization, and many more.

2. **Input Data Partition**: Split the whole input dataset into multiple chunks and assign each chunk to one accelerator for the model training process.

3. **Data Loading**: Load the data partition into the accelerators we use to train the model.

4. **Training**: Train the model locally with its training input data.

5. **Model Synchronization**: After generating the local gradient, synchronize it with the other worker nodes.

6. **Model Update**: After getting the synchronized gradients, update the local model parameters with the aggregated gradients.

7. Repeat *Steps 4* to *6* for the successive training iterations.

As shown in the preceding diagram, the main steps in data parallel training are training, model synchronization, and model updates, which are denoted by dark boxes. Now, let's discuss the implementation of each step.

Input pre-processing

For the input data pre-processing directly, we will use some pre-defined functions from the `torchvision` library, as follows:

```
import torch
...
from torchvision import transforms
```

We define our input pre-processing functions as follows:

```
# Transformations
RC = transforms.RandomCrop(32, padding=4)
RHF = transforms.RandomHorizontalFlip()
RVF = transforms.RandomVerticalFlip()
NRM = transforms.Normalize((0.1307,), (0.3081,))
TT = transforms.ToTensor()
TPIL = transforms.ToPILImage()
```

As shown in the preceding code snippet, we define six input pre-processing functions, which are as follows:

- `RC()` for image cropping and adding zero padding among the border of cropped images.
- `RHF()` for flipping the training image horizontally.
- `RVF()` for flipping the training image vertically.
- `NRM()` for normalizing a training image with mean and standard deviation. Note that the values for means and variance may vary for different datasets.
- `TT()` for transforming a `PIL` or `numpy` array into PyTorch tensor format.
- `TPIL()` for transforming a PyTorch tensor or a `numpy` array into a PIL image.

Once we have defined the pre-processing function, we can combine them to pre-process the training and test datasets, as follows:

```
# Transforms object for trainset with augmentation
transform_with_aug = transforms.Compose([RC, RHF, TT, NRM])
# Transforms object for testset with NO augmentation
transform_no_aug = transforms.Compose([TT, NRM])
```

As shown in the preceding code (`transform_with_aug`), for each training image, we pass it over `RC()`, `RHF()`, `TT()`, and `NRM()` sequentially.

For the test images, we will define `transform_no_aug()`, which only adds `TT()` and `NRM()` as the image pre-processing operations.

Then, we must wrap this up as a Python class for image pre-processing. The following code defines the pre-processing class for training the images:

```
class MNISTTrainingPreProcessing(...):
    def __init__(self, ...):
        dataset = datasets.MNIST(root=DATASET_ROOT,
        train=True,
                download=True,
                transform=transform_with_aug)
        super().__init__(dataset, ...)
```

For the test set, we must define a pre-processing Python class called `MNISTTestingPreProcessing()`, as shown in the following snippet:

```
class MNISTTestingPreProcessing(...):
    def __init__(self, ...):
        dataset = datasets.MNIST(root=DATASET_ROOT,
        train=False,
                download=True,
                transform=transform_with_no_aug)
        super().__init__(dataset, ...)
```

After performing image pre-processing, we need to split the input data into partitions and assign each partition to a worker for model training.

Input data partition

Compared to single-node training, data parallel training inserts this additional step into the training pipeline. Here, we directly borrow the `DistributedSampler()` function of PyTorch for training data distribution. It works as follows:

```
if args.distributed == True:
    train_partition = \
    torch.utils.data.distributed.DistributedSampler(train_set,...)
```

What this function does is scatter the whole training set into disjoint subsets. Thus, it guarantees that there are no duplicate images among those subsets.

Data loading

After getting the data partition for each GPU, we must load the training samples into the accelerators. On each GPU, we will define a `train_loader()` function, as follows:

```
train_loader = torch.utils.data.DataLoader(
                 trainset,
                 batch_size=args.train_batch,
        ...
                 num_workers=args.workers,
                 pin_memory=True)
```

Similarly, `test_loader()` uses the same function as `train_loader()`. We have omitted the detailed definition here.

One thing worth mentioning here is the `pin_memory` option. It is better to always set it to `True` if there is enough CPU memory. This is because pinned memory guarantees that the data stored in those memory pages will not be paged out. Thus, it guarantees the best data loading speed, from CPUs to devices.

Training

We assume that you have model training experience on a single node. In this section, we will highlight some key functions that are only used in data parallel training process.

First, we need to define our loss function:

```
import torch.nn as nn
loss_fn = nn.CrossEntropyLoss().cuda(device_i)
```

The loss function we normally use is `CrossEntropyLoss()`, which is quite popular for deep learning tasks. For simpler tasks, you may choose to use `MSELoss()` or `NLLLoss()` accordingly. `loss_function` and `criterion` are used interchangeably in PyTorch implementations.

Next, we need to define the optimizer for our data parallel training. As we discussed in *Chapter 1, Splitting Input Data*, we use **stochastic gradient descent (SGD)** as the main option for data parallel training. It is defined as follows:

```
import torch.optim
optimizer = torch.optim.SGD(model.parameters(),
    learning_rate, ...)
```

This code is fairly simple: we pass in `model.parameters()` and the related hyper-parameters (for example, `learning_rate`) into the SGD optimizer.

Model synchronization

After getting the data partition for each GPU, we must load the training samples into the accelerators. On each GPU, we must define a `train_loader()` function, as follows:

```
...
optimizer.zero_grad()
loss_fn.backward()
...
```

These steps cover the main backward propagation process. First, we zero out the gradients generated from the previous iteration. Second, we call the `backward()` function, which automatically performs model synchronization.

The model synchronization in `loss_fn.backward()` works as follows:

1. After a layer generates its local gradients, PyTorch initializes a per-layer All-Reduce function to get the globally synchronized gradients of this layer. To reduce the system control's overhead, PyTorch often groups multiple consequent layers and conducts a per-group All-Reduce function.

2. Once all the layers have finished their All-Reduce operations, PyTorch will write all the layers' gradients to the `gradient` space in `model_parameters()`. Note that this is a blocking function call, which means that the workers will not start further operations until the whole model's All-Reduce finishes.

After we've finished model synchronization among all the workers, we can allow each worker to update its local model parameters.

Model update

After model synchronization, each worker will update its local model parameters with the following `step()` function:

```
optimizer.step()
```

It is the same as the model update function in single-node training. Once the model has been updated, we can start the training iterations.

Single-machine multi-GPUs and multi-machine multi-GPUs

So far, we have discussed the main steps in data parallel training. In this section, we will explain two main types of hardware settings in data parallel training:

- The first type is *a single machine with multiple GPUs*. In this setting, all the in-parallel training tasks can be launched using either a single process or multiple processes.

- The second type is *multiple machines with multiple GPUs*. In this setting, we need to configure the network communication portals among all the machines. We also need to form a process group to synchronize both the cross-machine and cross-GPU training processes.

Single-machine multi-GPU

Compared to multi-machine multi-GPUs, the single-machine multiple-GPU setting is easier to set up. Before we discuss the implementation, let's check if the hardware configuration is good to go. Type the following command in the terminal:

```
$ nvidia-smi
```

If the NVIDIA driver and CUDA installation are correct, you should be able to see the following hardware information:

```
+-----------------------------------------------------------------------------+
| NVIDIA-SMI 450.119.03   Driver Version: 450.119.03   CUDA Version: 11.0     |
|-------------------------------+----------------------+----------------------+
| GPU  Name        Persistence-M| Bus-Id        Disp.A | Volatile Uncorr. ECC |
| Fan  Temp  Perf  Pwr:Usage/Cap|         Memory-Usage | GPU-Util  Compute M. |
|                               |                      |               MIG M. |
|===============================+======================+======================|
|   0  Tesla V100-SXM2...  On   | 00000000:00:1B.0 Off |                    0 |
| N/A   33C    P0    39W / 300W |      0MiB / 16160MiB |      0%      Default |
|                               |                      |                  N/A |
+-------------------------------+----------------------+----------------------+
|   1  Tesla V100-SXM2...  On   | 00000000:00:1C.0 Off |                    0 |
| N/A   33C    P0    39W / 300W |      0MiB / 16160MiB |      0%      Default |
|                               |                      |                  N/A |
+-------------------------------+----------------------+----------------------+
|   2  Tesla V100-SXM2...  On   | 00000000:00:1D.0 Off |                    0 |
| N/A   35C    P0    41W / 300W |      0MiB / 16160MiB |      0%      Default |
|                               |                      |                  N/A |
+-------------------------------+----------------------+----------------------+
|   3  Tesla V100-SXM2...  On   | 00000000:00:1E.0 Off |                    0 |
| N/A   35C    P0    41W / 300W |      0MiB / 16160MiB |      0%      Default |
|                               |                      |                  N/A |
+-------------------------------+----------------------+----------------------+

+-----------------------------------------------------------------------------+
| Processes:                                                                  |
|  GPU   GI   CI        PID   Type   Process name                  GPU Memory |
|        ID   ID                                                   Usage      |
|=============================================================================|
|  No running processes found                                                 |
+-----------------------------------------------------------------------------+
```

Figure 3.2 – NVIDIA-SMI information for a single-node multi-GPU

As we can see, for the hardware configuration, we use the NVIDIA driver version of 450.119.03 with a current CUDA version of 11.0. On this machine, we have four Tesla V100 GPUs, each of which has 16,160 MB (~16 GB) on-device memory.

For real-time system monitoring, type the following command in the terminal:

```
$ nvidia-smi stats
```

Then, the monitor can print out the GPU resource utilization in real time, which includes computation utilization (gpuUtil), memory utilization (memUtil), and many others.

We will assume that all the hardware configurations are correct. Now, let's jump into how data parallel training is done on a single machine with multiple GPUs.

First, we need to set the default device/accelerator in the system as follows:

```
import torch
device = torch.device ("cuda" if torch.cuda.is_available() else
"cpu")
```

Second, with our pre-defined model, we must pass the model to all the available devices, as follows:

```
model = torch.nn.DataParallel(model)
```

Then, PyTorch will conduct the data parallel training under the hood. When you run the whole data parallel training job, the system will launch a single process with multiple threads. Each thread is responsible for running training tasks on a single GPU. The whole workflow is as follows:

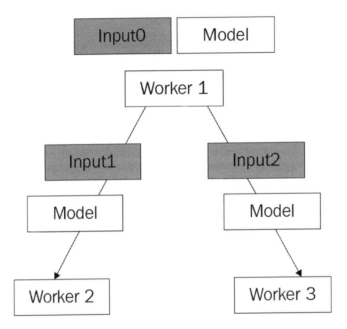

Figure 3.3 – Model and data partition distribution in nn.DataParallel()

As we can see, we set the default GPU to **Worker 1**. `nn.DataParallel()` works as follows:

1.   We initialize the model on **Worker 1** and let **Worker 1** split the input training data.

2.   **Worker 1** will broadcast the model parameters to all the other workers (that is, **Worker 2** and **Worker 3**). In addition, **Worker 1** will also send different input data partitions to different workers (**Input1** to **Worker 2**, and **Input2** to **Worker 3**).

3.   Then, we can start the data parallel training on all the devices.

During each training iteration, as shown in the following diagram, **Worker 1** needs to handle the extra operations, besides its local training:

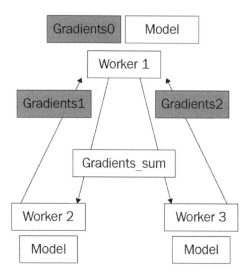

Figure 3.4 – Model synchronization in nn.DataParallel()

As we can see, after each worker generates its local gradients (for example, `Gradients0` on **Worker 1** and `Gradients1` on **Worker 2**), they will send their local gradients to **Worker 1**. After **Worker 1** aggregates all the gradients from all the workers as `Gradients_sum`, **Worker 1** will broadcast `Gradients_sum` to all the other workers.

Note that the `Gradients_sum` broadcast is equivalent to broadcasting the updated model. As an alternative option, the real system implementation can be all the workers pulling the updated model from the default worker.

One way to check whether this data parallel training job uses multiple GPUs is by printing out the `nvidis-smi` information. As shown in the following screenshot, if the job is being successfully run using `nn.DataParallel()`, you may find that all the GPUs are being used and that they share the same process ID (`7906` in the following screenshot):

```
+-----------------------------------------------------------------------------+
| Processes:                                                                  |
|  GPU   GI   CI        PID   Type   Process name                 GPU Memory  |
|        ID   ID                                                  Usage       |
|=============================================================================|
|    0   N/A  N/A      7906     C   python                            1393MiB |
|    1   N/A  N/A      7906     C   python                            1393MiB |
|    2   N/A  N/A      7906     C   python                            1393MiB |
|    3   N/A  N/A      7906     C   python                            1035MiB |
+-----------------------------------------------------------------------------+
```

Figure 3.5 – Checking the GPU running status of a data parallel job using nn.DataParallel()

Furthermore, you can also specify the devices you want to use by specifying another argument as `device_ids`. For example, if you just want to use two GPUs inside your machine, you can pass in the parameters like so:

```
model = torch.nn.DataParallel(model, device_ids=[0,1])
```

Here, you just use two GPUs (GPU0 and GPU1) for this data parallel training job.

> **Important Note**
> In terms of single-machine multiple-GPUs, we can launch just one process with multi-threading. Each thread is responsible for running local training tasks on a single GPU.

As we described previously, the implementation of `nn.DataParallel()` involves a lot of all-to-one and one-to-all communications, which makes the default root node become the communication bottleneck. Thus, we should adopt a scheme that evenly distributes the workloads and network communications.

In addition, the PyTorch user manual suggests that due to the **global interpreter lock (GIL)** issue inherit from Python, multi-processing can be a better option for launching data parallel training jobs.

Next, we will illustrate how to implement data parallel training with multi-processing.

Multi-machine multi-GPU

In this section, we will discuss multi-process implementations for multiple machines cases. The machines we will use have the same number of GPUs, though this is not necessary. Before we jump into the implementation, we need to define some concepts for multi-machine cases:

- `rank`: A unique sequence number for all the GPUs in all the machines
- `local_rank`: A sequence number for the GPUs within a machine
- `world_size`: A count of all the GPUs in all the machines, which is just the total number of GPUs among all the machines

A simple example is illustrated in the following diagram. Here, we have two machines, each with two GPUs. `local_rank` for two GPUs within each machine can be 0 or 1. Rank numbers are unique per GPU among all the machines. In the following diagram, the rank number ranges from 0 to 3. Since there are four GPUs in total, `world_size` is **4**:

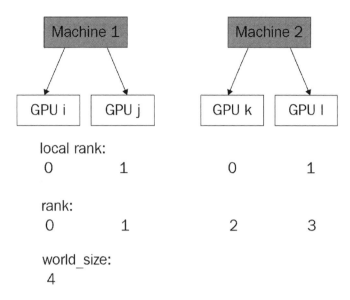

Figure 3.6 – Illustration of local rank, rank, and world_size in distributed data parallel training

Instead of using `nn.DataParallel()` here, we use `nn.parallel.DistributedDataParallel()`:

```
from torch.nn.parallel import DistributedDataParallel as DDP
```

We also need to import other relevant libraries for distributed data parallel training, as shown in the following snippet:

```
import torch.distributed as dist
import torch.distributed.autograd as dist_autograd
from torchvision import datasets, transforms
from torch import optim
from torch.distributed.optim import DistributedOptimizer
from torch.nn.parallel import DistributedDataParallel as DDP
from torch.utils.data.distributed import DistributedSampler as DDP_sampler
```

Finally, we must import torch's multi-processing library, as follows:

```
import torch.multiprocessing as mp
```

In multi-processing mode, we need to define several system setups, as follows:

1. We need to set up the network environments for the master node:

```
import os
def net_setup():
    os.environ['MASTER_ADDR'] = '172.31.26.15'
    os.environ['MASTER_PORT'] = '12345'
```

As shown here, we need to set up the master node's IP address and port number.

2. We must also parse some important parameters from the user, as follows:

```
def main():
    ...
    parser = argparse.ArgumentParser(description =
'distributed data parallel training')
    parser.add_argument('-m', '--machines', default=2,
type=int, help='number of machines')
    parser.add_argument('-g', '--gpus', default = 4,
type=int, help='number of GPUs in a machine')
    parser.add_argument('-id', '--mid', default = 0,
type=int, help='machine id number')
    parser.add_argument('-e', '--epochs', default = 2,
type = int, help='number of epochs')
```

Here, we need to parse the number of machines in this data parallel training job (that is, '--machines'), the number of GPUs within each machine (that is, '--gpus'), the current machine ID (that is, '--mid'), and the number of epochs for the training process (that is, '--epochs').

3. We must use PyTorch multi-processing to spawn processes:

```
mp.spawn(train, nprocs=args.gpus, args=(args,),
join=True)
```

This launches multiple processes where each process is responsible for training tasks on a single GPU.

↳ apply in MTL

After performing these steps, we need to define our distributed training function. Here, we will only highlight the new functions that have been introduced in this multi-process data parallel training process:

- Set `torch_seed` while calculating `global_rank` and `world_size`:

```
def train(local_rank, args):
    torch.manual_seed(123)
    world_size = args.machines * args.gpus
    rank = args.mid * args.gpus + local_rank
```

We can define the training function with the following key components:

  - `manual_seed` is used to guarantee that we initialize the same model weights among all the worker nodes we have.

  - `world_size` is defined as the multiplication of the number of machines and the number of GPUs within a machine.

  - `rank` is calculated as the global rank number for a specific GPU.

- Initialize the process group with the communication backend:

```
dist.init_process_group('nccl',
            rank =rank,
            world_size = world_size,
                    timeout=datetime.
    timedelta(seconds=60))
```

Here, we use NCCL as our communication backend, though you may wish to choose other communication backends (for example, `'gloo'`), such as the ones we introduced in *Chapter 1, Splitting Input Data*.

- Add `sampler` to `data_loader`:

```
local_train_loader = \
torch.utils.data.DataLoader(datasets.MNIST('./mnist_
data',
            download=True,
        train=True,
                transform = ...
                    shuffle = False,
                    sampler = local_train_sampler)
```

As we can see, we are passing `DataLoader` in with the dataset and our pre-defined `local_train_sampler()`. The `local_train_sampler()` function is introduced in the input data partition section.

- Wrap the model with `DistributedDataParallel()`

```
model = DDP(model,
        device_ids=[local_rank])
```

Here, we wrap our model in DDP (that is, `DistributedDataParallel`) mode and each GPU's `local_rank` number.

With all these setups added to our `train()` function, we can train the model, similar to what we did for single-node training. The core piece of code for this training process is as follows:

```
for epoch in range(args.epochs):
    print(f"Epoch {epoch}")
    for idx, (data, target) in enumerate(local_train_loader):
        data = data.cuda()
        target = target.cuda()
        output = model(data)
        loss = F.cross_entropy(output, target)
        loss.backward()
        optimizer.step()
```

With that, we have finished implementing multi-processing data parallel training in multi-machine, multi-GPU settings.

To launch this distributed training job correctly, open a terminal on each machine and type in the following commands:

- For the master machine with an IP of `172.31.26.15`, use the following command:

```
ubuntu@172-31-26-15$ python main.py --mid=0
```

- For the other machine with an IP of `172.31.26.16`, use the following command:

```
ubuntu@172-31-26-16$ python main.py --mid=1
```

You can add additional machines to this data parallel training workload by setting `--mid` to additional numbers.

Here, we used two machines each with four GPUs. When you successfully run the preceding scripts, you will see concurrent training on each machine, as follows:

```
ubuntu@172-31-26-16$ python main.py --mid=0
Epoch 0
Epoch 0
Epoch 0
Epoch 0
batch 0 training :: loss 2.3160948753356934
batch 0 training :: loss 2.3030762672424316
batch 0 training :: loss 2.3058559894561768
batch 0 training :: loss 2.3034820556640625
batch 1 training :: loss 2.3026175498962402
batch 1 training :: loss 2.313504695892334
batch 1 training :: loss 2.306662082672119
batch 1 training :: loss 2.311518907546997
...
batch 56 training :: loss 0.359452486038208
batch 56 training :: loss 0.3805597722530365
batch 56 training :: loss 0.2707654535770416
batch 56 training :: loss 0.4161689281463623
batch 57 training :: loss 0.22238844633102417
batch 57 training :: loss 0.38648080825805664
batch 57 training :: loss 0.305296391248703
batch 57 training :: loss 0.3957134783267975
batch 58 training :: loss 0.3631390929222107
Training Done!
batch 58 training :: loss 0.38556599617004395
batch 58 training :: loss 0.45669931173324585
Training Done!
Training Done!
batch 58 training :: loss 0.20888786017894745
Training Done!
```

As we can see, we have four GPUs concurrently training on the same machines. Given that we have *eight GPUs* in total (two machines), with batch sizes of 128, each GPU only needs to train ~58 mini-batches of training data for 1 epoch of training. This is around *1/8* the number of batches in single-node training mode.

In addition, since we use multi-processing for concurrent model training on multiple machines, as shown in *Figure 3.7* and *Figure 3.8*, both machines are running four different processes, each on one GPU.

For example, on the master machine (*Figure 3.7*), we launch processes 40074 to 40077 on four different GPUs. On the other four-GPU machine (*Figure 3.8*), we have processes 27914-27917 on the other four GPUs.

Compared to `DataParallel()` in PyTorch, `DistributedDataParallel()` has better load balancing among all the workers. As shown in *Figure 3.7* and *Figure 3.8*, all the GPUs have similar memory footprints and computation core utilizations. This indicates that the workload is evenly distributed among all the workers. Thus, all the GPUs can finish their training job at roughly the same time, which means there are no stragglers in the whole parallel system:

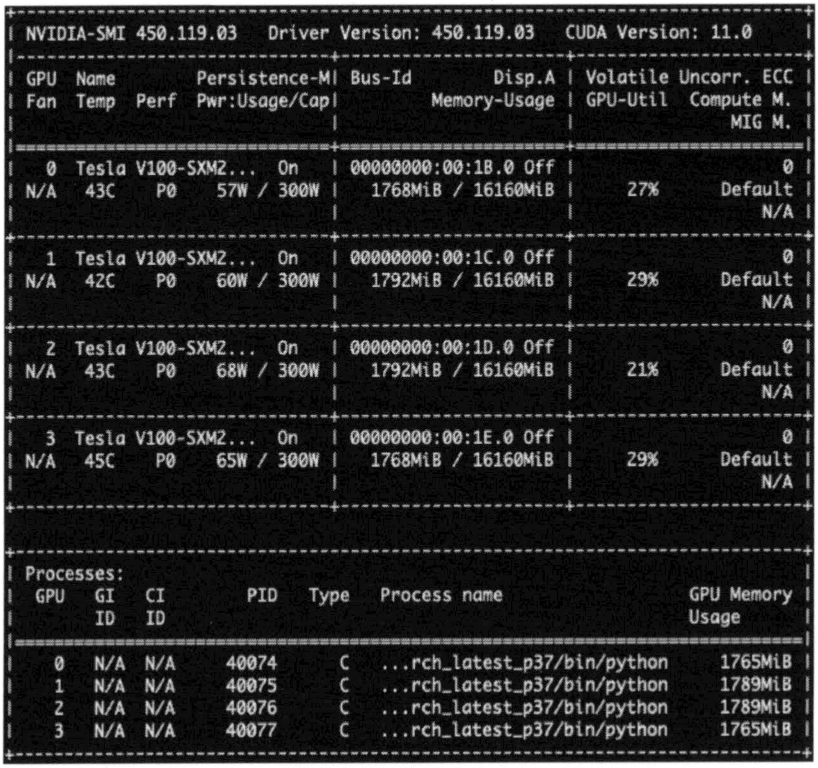

```
+-----------------------------------------------------------------------------+
| NVIDIA-SMI 450.119.03   Driver Version: 450.119.03   CUDA Version: 11.0      |
|-------------------------------+----------------------+----------------------+
| GPU  Name        Persistence-M| Bus-Id        Disp.A | Volatile Uncorr. ECC |
| Fan  Temp  Perf  Pwr:Usage/Cap|         Memory-Usage | GPU-Util  Compute M. |
|                               |                      |               MIG M. |
|===============================+======================+======================|
|   0  Tesla V100-SXM2...  On   | 00000000:00:1B.0 Off |                    0 |
| N/A   43C    P0    57W / 300W |   1768MiB / 16160MiB |     27%      Default |
|                               |                      |                  N/A |
+-------------------------------+----------------------+----------------------+
|   1  Tesla V100-SXM2...  On   | 00000000:00:1C.0 Off |                    0 |
| N/A   42C    P0    60W / 300W |   1792MiB / 16160MiB |     29%      Default |
|                               |                      |                  N/A |
+-------------------------------+----------------------+----------------------+
|   2  Tesla V100-SXM2...  On   | 00000000:00:1D.0 Off |                    0 |
| N/A   43C    P0    68W / 300W |   1792MiB / 16160MiB |     21%      Default |
|                               |                      |                  N/A |
+-------------------------------+----------------------+----------------------+
|   3  Tesla V100-SXM2...  On   | 00000000:00:1E.0 Off |                    0 |
| N/A   45C    P0    65W / 300W |   1768MiB / 16160MiB |     29%      Default |
|                               |                      |                  N/A |
+-------------------------------+----------------------+----------------------+

+-----------------------------------------------------------------------------+
| Processes:                                                                  |
|  GPU   GI   CI        PID   Type   Process name                  GPU Memory |
|        ID   ID                                                    Usage      |
|=============================================================================|
|    0   N/A  N/A     40074     C   ...rch_latest_p37/bin/python     1765MiB  |
|    1   N/A  N/A     40075     C   ...rch_latest_p37/bin/python     1789MiB  |
|    2   N/A  N/A     40076     C   ...rch_latest_p37/bin/python     1789MiB  |
|    3   N/A  N/A     40077     C   ...rch_latest_p37/bin/python     1765MiB  |
+-----------------------------------------------------------------------------+
```

Figure 3.7 – The running status of the master machine

As shown in *Figure 3.7* and *Figure 3.8*, all the GPUs have computation core utilities of around 20-30%, and their memory consumption is around 1,800 MB each.

In comparison, as shown in *Figure 3.3* and *Figure 3.4*, for `DataParallel()` with a single process, GPU 0 (**Worker 1**) has more of a computation workload. The extra workload includes gradient aggregation and input data distribution, and so on. So, this makes GPU 0 (**Worker 1**) the bottleneck and straggler in this data parallel training job:

```
+-----------------------------------------------------------------------------+
| NVIDIA-SMI 450.142.00   Driver Version: 450.142.00   CUDA Version: 11.0     |
|-------------------------------+----------------------+----------------------+
| GPU  Name        Persistence-M| Bus-Id        Disp.A | Volatile Uncorr. ECC |
| Fan  Temp  Perf  Pwr:Usage/Cap|         Memory-Usage | GPU-Util  Compute M. |
|                               |                      |               MIG M. |
|===============================+======================+======================|
|   0  Tesla V100-SXM2...  On   | 00000000:00:1B.0 Off |                    0 |
| N/A   45C    P0    71W / 300W |   1768MiB / 16160MiB |     25%      Default |
|                               |                      |                  N/A |
+-------------------------------+----------------------+----------------------+
|   1  Tesla V100-SXM2...  On   | 00000000:00:1C.0 Off |                    0 |
| N/A   46C    P0    67W / 300W |   1792MiB / 16160MiB |     24%      Default |
|                               |                      |                  N/A |
+-------------------------------+----------------------+----------------------+
|   2  Tesla V100-SXM2...  On   | 00000000:00:1D.0 Off |                    0 |
| N/A   47C    P0    82W / 300W |   1792MiB / 16160MiB |     26%      Default |
|                               |                      |                  N/A |
+-------------------------------+----------------------+----------------------+
|   3  Tesla V100-SXM2...  On   | 00000000:00:1E.0 Off |                    0 |
| N/A   45C    P0    73W / 300W |   1768MiB / 16160MiB |     29%      Default |
|                               |                      |                  N/A |
+-------------------------------+----------------------+----------------------+

+-----------------------------------------------------------------------------+
| Processes:                                                                  |
|  GPU   GI   CI        PID   Type   Process name               GPU Memory    |
|        ID   ID                                                Usage         |
|=============================================================================|
|    0   N/A  N/A     27914     C   ...rch_latest_p37/bin/python     1765MiB   |
|    1   N/A  N/A     27915     C   ...rch_latest_p37/bin/python     1789MiB   |
|    2   N/A  N/A     27916     C   ...rch_latest_p37/bin/python     1789MiB   |
|    3   N/A  N/A     27917     C   ...rch_latest_p37/bin/python     1765MiB   |
+-----------------------------------------------------------------------------+
```

Figure 3.8 – The running status of the other worker machine

Therefore, for a data parallel training job, it is better to use the multi-process `DistributedDataParallel()` than the single-process `DataParallel()`. The main reason for this is twofold:

- `DistributedDataParallel()` has better load balancing than `DataParallel()`.

- `DistributedDataParallel()` has less one-to-all and all-to-one communications than `DataParallel()`. Thus, it mitigates the communication bottleneck issue in `DataParallel()`.

In the next section, we will discuss how to add fault tolerance to data parallelism pipelines.

Checkpointing and fault tolerance

Previously, we discussed two different implementations of data parallel training, namely `DistributedDataParallel()` and `DataParallel()`.

One thing we are missing here is fault tolerance, which is important in distributed systems.

Since `DistributedDataParallel()` is better than `DataParallel()`, we will illustrate our checkpointing implementation in `DistributedDataParallel()` setting. In this setting, each process is responsible for checkpointing a model from one GPU.

Model checkpointing

First, we will discuss how we can achieve in-parallel model saving, also known as model checkpointing.

The checkpointing function in the multi-processing setting is defined as follows:

```
def checkpointing(rank, epoch, net, optimizer, loss):
    path = f"model{rank}.pt"
    torch.save({
        'epoch':epoch,
        'model_state':net.state_dict(),
        'loss': loss,
        'optim_state': optimizer.state_dict(),
        }, path)
    print(f"Checkpointing model {rank} done.")
```

For each process, we use its global ranking number to create the model saving path (that is, `f"model{rank}.pt"`). Using the global ranking number in the path name guarantees that two processes can't be saved to the same path address.

Once the path has been created, we save the loss, epoch number, model, and optimizer parameters using `torch.save()` to the path we defined.

After each training iteration, we can save a model checkpoint for fault tolerance.

Load model checkpoints

When some machines go down, we need to load the models that were previously checkpointed. We can define our multi-process checkpoint loading function as follows:

```
def load_checkpoint(rank, machines):
  path = f"model{rank}.pt"
  checkpoint = torch.load(path)
  model = torch.nn.DataParallel(MyNet(),
                        device_ids=[rank%machines])
  optimizer = torch.optim.SGD(model.parameters(),
          lr = 5e-4)
  ...
  epoch = checkpoint['epoch']
  loss = checkpoint['loss']
  model.load_state_dict(checkpoint['model_state'])
  optimizer.load_state_dict(checkpoint['optim_state'])
      return model, optimizer, epoch, loss
```

We allow each process to load its own saved model using the same path naming rule (that is, `path = f"model{rank}.pt"`) as the `checkpointing()` function.

Then, we load epoch number, loss, model weights, and the optimizer one by one via the checkpoint we loaded.

Note that, in the `DistributedDataParallel()` setting, our model is wrapped with `DDP()`, which keeps the model as a PyTorch `module`. To successfully load the model parameters, we need to define our model in the PyTorch `module` by wrapping it as `torch.nn.DataParallel(MyNet(), device_ids=[rank%machines])`. Note that we also need to assign the loaded model into the correct `device_id`, which is calculated as `rank%machines` here.

After defining both the save and load functions for multi-processing checkpointing, we can insert them into our training function. Then, we can launch a multi-processing data parallel training job, as shown in the following terminal output.

On the master machine, it prints the following:

```
...
batch 58 training :: loss 0.5455576777458191
batch 58 training :: loss 0.7072545886039734
batch 58 training :: loss 0.953201174736023
```

```
batch 58 training :: loss 0.512895941734314
Checkpointing model 2 done.
Training Done!
Load checkpoint 2
Checkpointing model 1 done.
Training Done!
Load checkpoint 1
Checkpointing model 0 done.
Checkpointing model 3 done.
Training Done!
Load checkpoint 0
Training Done!
Load checkpoint 3
Checkpoint loading done!
Checkpoint loading done!
Checkpoint loading done!
Checkpoint loading done!
```

On the other four-GPU worker machine, it concurrently outputs similar results, as follows:

```
...
batch 58 training :: loss 0.7266647815704346
batch 58 training :: loss 0.5634446144104004
batch 58 training :: loss 0.5879226922988892
batch 58 training :: loss 0.5659951567649841
Checkpointing model 6 done.
Training Done!
Load checkpoint 6
Checkpointing model 7 done.
Training Done!
Load checkpoint 7
Checkpointing model 5 done.
Training Done!
Load checkpoint 5
Checkpoint loading done!
Checkpoint loading done!
```

```
Checkpoint loading done!
Checkpointing model 4 done.
Training Done!
Load checkpoint 4
Checkpoint loading done!
```

As you can see, the master machine will save and load models 0 to 3. The other four-GPU worker will save and load models 4 to7. This tells us that all our in-parallel saved checkpoints can be distinguished from each other using the global ranking number.

The preceding output suggests that we can successfully save and load our model checkpoints in a multi-processing setting.

Adding this checkpointing feature guarantees that we can achieve fault tolerance in distributed training environments.

Model evaluation and hyperparameter tuning

After each epoch of our data parallel model training, we need to evaluate whether the training progress is good or not. We use these evaluation results to conduct hyperparameter tuning, such as the learning rate and batch size per GPU.

Note that the validation set for hyper parameter tuning is from the training set, not the test set, so we split the total training data with a *5:1* ratio. *5/6* of the total training data is for model training, while *1/6* of the total data is for model validation. This can be implemented as follows:

```
train_all_set = datasets.MNIST('./mnist_data',
        download=True, train=True,
            transform = transforms.Compose([
        transforms.ToTensor(),
            transforms.Normalize((0.1307,),
            (0.3081,))]))
train_set, val_set = torch.utils.data.random_split(
            train_all_set,
                [50000, 10000])
```

Here, we define the whole training set as `train_all_set`.

Then, we split the whole training set into `train_set` and `val_set` via `torch.utils.data.random_split()` with a ratio of 5:1.

After getting our `val_set`, we must define our `validation` function, as follows:

```python
def validation(model, val_set):
    model.eval()
    val_loader = torch.utils.data.DataLoader(val_set,
            batch_size=128)
    correct_total = 0
    with torch.no_grad():
        for idx, (data, target) in enumerate(val_loader):
            output = model(data)
            predict = output.argmax(dim=1,
                    keepdim=True).cuda()
            target = target.cuda()
            correct =\
            predict.eq(target.view_as(predict)).sum().item()
            correct_total += correct
        acc = correct_total/len(val_loader.dataset)
    print(f"Validation Accuracy {acc}")
```

We carried out the following steps in the preceding code:

1. First, we used the `model.eval()` flag to turn this model into evaluation mode.

2. The `torch.no_grad()` function guarantees that we will not need to generate gradients for the model update.

3. We calculate the corresponding validation accuracy by conducting a forward pass of the validation data on the model weights.

4. We insert this validation function into the training function. After each epoch of training, we need to test the validation accuracy to see if the model is making good training progress and adjust the hyperparameters accordingly.

In multi-processing training mode, you will see the following validation evaluation results after each epoch of training:

```
...
batch 58 training :: loss 1.040719985961914
batch 58 training :: loss 1.1270662546157837
batch 58 training :: loss 1.5198094844818115
batch 58 training :: loss 1.0102834701538086
Checkpointing model 1 done.
Checkpointing model 2 done.
Checkpointing model 0 done.
Checkpointing model 3 done.
Validation Accuracy 0.671
Training Done!
Load checkpoint 0
Validation Accuracy 0.6754
Training Done!
Load checkpoint 2
Checkpoint loading done!
Checkpoint loading done!
Validation Accuracy 0.6663
Training Done!
Load checkpoint 1
Checkpoint loading done!
Validation Accuracy 0.6698
Training Done!
Load checkpoint 3
Checkpoint loading done!
```

With the validation accuracy done after each training iteration; we can use these values to conduct hyperparameter tuning for our data parallel training job. For example, if the validation accuracy grows too slowly, we may change the learning rate to a larger value or enlarge the batch size of each GPU.

Note that if we have massive computational power, we can try different hyperparameters simultaneously, as shown in the following diagram:

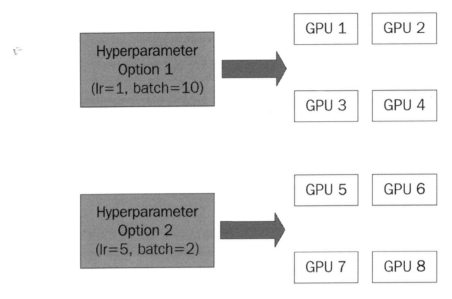

Figure 3.9 – Concurrent hyperparameter tuning using massive accelerators

With a large number of GPUs, we can conduct concurrent hyperparameter tuning on different groups of accelerators.

For example, in the preceding diagram, given that we have two hyperparameter options (option 1 and option 2), we can run a data parallel training job using GPUs 1 to 4 with hyperparameter option 1. Simultaneously, we can run another data parallel training job on GPUs 5 to 8 using hyperparameter option 2.

After several training iterations, based on the validation accuracy we calculated in the previous section, we can keep the data parallel training job with the good hyperparameter option. Here, good means that it has higher validation accuracy. On the other hand, we can shut down the data parallel training job with the bad hyperparameter option and try using a new hyperparameter setting on this group of accelerators.

Model serving in data parallelism

So far, we have discussed the whole training pipeline via data parallelism. We will now illustrate the implementation details of data parallel serving.

First, we need to define our test dataset:

```
test_set = datasets.MNIST('./mnist_data', download=True,
train=False,
     transform =
       transforms.Compose([transforms.ToTensor(),
            transforms.Normalize((0.1307,),(0.3081,))]))
```

Next, we need to load the trained models into our GPUs using the `load_checkpoint()` function, which we defined previously.

Then, we need to define our in-parallel model test function, as follows:

```
def test(local_rank, args):
    world_size = args.machines*args.gpus
    rank = args.mid * args.gpus + local_rank
    ...
    torch.cuda.set_device(local_rank)
    ...
    model, optimizer, epoch, loss = load_checkpoint(rank,
              args.machines)
    ...
    local_test_sampler = DDP_sampler(test_set, rank = rank,
num_replicas = world_size)
    ...
    model.eval()
    local_test_loader = torch.utils.data.DataLoader(\
test_set,
                                    batch_size=128
                                    shuffle = False,
          sampler = local_test_sampler)
    correct_total = 0
    with torch.no_grad():
    ...
        acc = correct_total/len(local_test_loader.dataset)
```

```
print(f"GPU {rank}, Test Accuracy {acc}")
print("Test Done!")
dist.destroy_process_group()
```

In the preceding in-parallel test/serving function, the following steps were conducted:

1. Each model checkpoint was loaded into one particular GPU.

2. The sample test data was passed to different GPUs.

3. The test accuracy was calculated concurrently among all the GPUs.

Now that we have our in-parallel test function definition, we can use it for data parallel model inference in a multi-machine with multi-GPU settings. The following screenshot shows a data parallel inference job running on two machines, each with four GPUs:

```
Load checkpoint 3          Load checkpoint 6
Load checkpoint 2          Load checkpoint 5
Load checkpoint 1          Load checkpoint 7
Load checkpoint 0          Load checkpoint 4
Checkpoint loading done!   Checkpoint loading done!
Checkpoint loading done!   Checkpoint loading done!
GPU 0, Test Accuracy 0.1198   GPU 5, Test Accuracy 0.119
Test Done!                 Test Done!
GPU 1, Test Accuracy 0.1189   GPU 4, Test Accuracy 0.1202
Test Done!                 Test Done!
Checkpoint loading done!   Checkpoint loading done!
Checkpoint loading done!   Checkpoint loading done!
GPU 2, Test Accuracy 0.1192   GPU 7, Test Accuracy 0.1195
Test Done!                 Test Done!
GPU 3, Test Accuracy 0.1181   GPU 6, Test Accuracy 0.1193
Test Done!                 Test Done!
```

Figure 3.10 – In-parallel model serving in a multi-machine with multi-GPU settings

It is worth mentioning that checkpoint loading is not always in the same order. As shown in the preceding screenshot, model loading is done in a random order for both the left-hand side and right-hand side machines. For example, on the right of the preceding screenshot, the model loading order is **6, 5, 7, 4**. This random order model loading is due to concurrency and will not have any impact on the in-parallel model inference job.

Summary

In this chapter, we discussed how to implement a model training and serving pipeline using the data parallelism paradigm.

First, we illustrated the whole data parallel training pipeline and defined the key functions in each step. Then, we showed the implementation of data parallel training in both single-machine multi-GPUs and multi-machine multi-GPUs. We concluded that this multi-process implementation is better than a single process with multi-threading. Then, we discussed adding the fault tolerance feature to a data parallel training job. After that, we showed you how to conduct in-parallel model evaluation and hyperparameter tuning. Finally, we demonstrated how to implement data parallel model serving.

In the next chapter, we will discuss the bottlenecks in the current solutions for data parallelism. We will also provide solutions that can mitigate these bottleneck issues and boost end-to-end performance.

4
Bottlenecks and Solutions

Using the code we designed in *Chapter 3, Building a Data Parallel Training and Serving Pipeline*, we can build data parallel training and serving pipelines using either the parameter server or the All-Reduce paradigm. Similar to what we did in *Chapter 3, Building a Data Parallel Training and Serving Pipeline*, in this chapter, we will focus on the more widely used **All-Reduce paradigm**.

In this chapter, we will discuss the shortcomings in the current data parallel training and serving pipelines. For practical system bottleneck discussions, we will make the following assumptions:

- We use homogenous accelerators for all our model training nodes.

- Compared to CPU memory (that is, main memory), the on-device memory for each accelerator is limited.

- In multi-GPU, multi-machine cases, the cross-machine network bandwidth is significantly lower than the communication bandwidth among GPUs within a single machine.

- The training job is exclusively running on the machines. This means that the CPU computation cores and CPU memory are likely to be idle when performing model training on the GPUs of the machines.

- For a single machine, copying data between the host CPU and GPU is slower than transferring data among GPUs.

- For accelerators such as GPUs, the GPU memory is rarer than the GPU computation cores. Therefore, we may tend to trade computation resources for a smaller on-device memory footprint. 🐌

With the preceding assumptions in mind, we will talk about the bottlenecks of data parallel training in two dimensions: **on-device memory** and **communication network**. First, we will discuss the communication bottleneck issue in the data parallel training process. This communication bottleneck is more pronounced in cross-machine cases. Then, we will describe the state-of-the-art solutions for mitigating these communication bottlenecks. After that, we will analyze the memory wall issue in data parallel training. Finally, we will provide some classic solutions that can help mitigate this on-device memory limitation.

In a nutshell, the following topics will be covered in this chapter:

- Communication bottlenecks in data parallel training

- Leveraging idle links and host resources

- On-device memory bottlenecks

- Recomputation and quantization

Communication bottlenecks in data parallel training

As we mentioned in *Chapter 2*, *Parameter Server and All-Reduce*, and *Chapter 3*, *Building a Data Parallel Training and Serving Pipeline*, we need to conduct a communication-heavy step, namely **model synchronization**, after each training iteration.

In this section, we will conduct the theoretical analysis for the total traffic needs that are to be transferred over the network. Then, we will identify network inefficiency in widely used communication protocols such as **NCCL** and **Gloo**.

Analyzing the communication workloads

Let's dive into this communication-heavy step a little deeper. The model synchronization step is performed for the following purposes:

- Aggregating all the gradients that have been generated from all the workers

- Updating the model weights of all the workers

Some notations that will be used in this section are as follows:

- g_i: The local gradients that are generated from a single worker
- G: The globally synchronized gradients
- W: The number of parameters for the model weights
- N: The total number of workers
- BW_node: The cross-machine communication bandwidth
- BW_gpu: The pairwise GPU communication bandwidth within a single machine

Now, let's dive into the details of communication workloads in the parameter server and All-Reduce architectures.

Parameter server architecture

For the **parameter server architecture**, we will simplify our analysis by regarding all the sharded parameter servers as a whole unit. Therefore, we will only calculate the communication traffic between the parameter servers and all the worker nodes.

For *Step 1* of aggregating gradients from all the workers, we have a unidirectional traffic flow from the workers to the parameter servers, as shown in the following diagram:

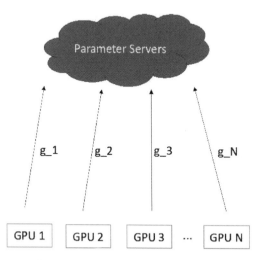

Figure 4.1 – Gradients aggregation in the parameter server architecture

The total amount of data that needs to be transferred here is as follows:

$$N * g\_i \quad (i \in 1...N)$$

Note that all the workers have the same number of gradients to transfer, which means the following:

$$g\_1 = g\_2 = \ldots = g\_n$$

Thus, we simplify our notation for *Step 1* communication traffic as follows:

$$N * g$$

Let's assume that each machine only has one GPU, so the cross-machine bandwidth is *BW_node*. We assume that we have *M* parameter servers for load balancing, where *M<=N*. Therefore, the total time for transferring data in *Step 1* communication (that is, *t1*) is as follows:

$$t1 = \frac{N * g}{M * BW\_node}$$

After *Step 1* communication, the parameter workers will aggregate all the gradients from all the workers together, which is illustrated as follows:

$$G = g\_1 + g\_2 + \ldots + g\_n$$

After this gradient aggregation, the parameter servers will update the model weights locally on each server. Then, we have our second communication step, which is updating the model weights on the worker nodes.

Step 2 of the communication process also concerns unidirectional network traffic from the parameter servers to all the workers, as shown in the following diagram:

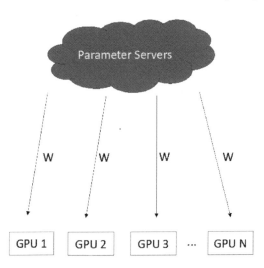

Figure 4.2 – Model updates in the parameter server architecture

As we can see, all the workers pull the model weights from the parameter servers simultaneously. Each worker needs to pull the amount of data traffic equal to W, which is the total number of weights in the model.

Therefore, the total amount of data traffic in *Step 2* is as follows:

$$N * W$$

Usually, the data size of the weights (that is, W) and the data size of the gradients (for example, g_i) are similar. However, the total amount of weights is often slightly larger than the total number of gradients, since some model layers do not generate gradients during backward propagation.

We also make a similar assumption as *Step 1* of communication. We assume that there are M parameter servers ($M<=N$) and that each worker has a single GPU. Thus, the total time to transfer the data in our second step (that is, $t2$) is as follows:

$$t2 = \frac{N * W}{M * BW\_node}$$

In summary, the total time to complete model synchronization in the parameter server architecture is as follows:

$$t\_ps = t1 + t2$$

Key Points to Remember

The time consumption of model synchronization in the parameter server architecture is as follows:

Step 1 involves aggregating the gradient time ($t1$):

$$t1 = \frac{N * g}{M * BW\_node}$$

Step 2 involves updating the model time ($t2$):

$$t2 = \frac{N * W}{M * BW\_node}$$

So, the total time for model synchronization is as follows:

$$t\_ps = t1 + t2$$

Note that here, $t1$ and $t2$ cannot be overlapped, which means that all the GPUs need to wait for $t1+t2$ time; the model synchronization time cannot be shrunk down to less than $t1+t2$.

This model synchronization overhead is added to each training iteration. As reported by state-of-the-art research literature, the time cost for model synchronization can be up to 50% of the end-to-end DNN training time if we scale out to more than 50 GPUs. Therefore, this communication overhead is huge and makes GPU computation cores idle for 50% of the total training time.

The All-Reduce architecture

Now, let's discuss the communication overhead in the All-Reduce architecture. In the All-Reduce architecture, all the nodes are workers. The gradient synchronization happens among all the workers. In this section, we will discuss the **Ring All-Reduce protocol**. For more details, please refer to *Chapter 2, Parameter Server and All-Reduce*. To simplify the case, we will limit our discussion to a single-machine, multi-GPU case. It is equivalent to a multi-machine, single-GPU case (the only difference is changing BW_gpu to BW_node). It can easily extend to a multi-machine, multi-GPU case.

Let's look at a simple case, as shown in the following diagram, where we have three GPUs connected in a **ring topology**. Each link has a bidirectional communication bandwidth of BW_gpu:

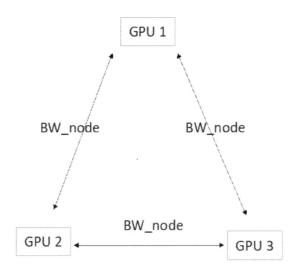

Figure 4.3 – Network topology in a simple All-Reduce architecture

The All-Reduce architecture requires two steps of communication to finish model synchronization, as follows:

1. Reduce from a root node and get the aggregated gradients back to the root node.

2. Broadcast the aggregated gradients.

Let's discuss these communication steps one by one.

For the time consumption of the first step, given N workers, we need to forward the data size of g_i N times. Similar to the previous parameter server analysis, we also assume the following:

$$g_1 = g_2 = \ldots = g_n$$

Then, we abstract all the g_i data sizes so that they're g. Next, we will talk about *Step-1 Reduce*, as shown in the following diagram:

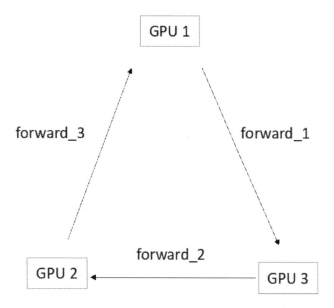

Figure 4.4 - Step-1 Reduce in the All-Reduce architecture

Let's illustrate the preceding conclusion of N times forwarding in our three-GPU example. As shown in the preceding diagram, *Step-1 Reduce* works as follows:

1. **GPU 1** sends its local gradient, *g_1*, to **GPU 2** (**forward_1**).
2. **GPU 2** aggregates its local gradient, *g_2*, with **GPU 1's** *g_1*, then sends *g_1+g_2* to **GPU 3** (**forward_2**).
3. **GPU 3** aggregates its local gradient, *g_3*, with *g_1+g_2*, then sends *g_1+g_2+g_3* to **GPU 1** (**forward_3**).

For N GPUs, it still follows the preceding workflow as the *Step-1* Reduce process. Thus, given N GPUs in use, we need to conduct N-*times* forwarding. The time for this N-*times* forwarding is as follows:

$$t1 = \frac{N * g}{BW\_gpu}$$

Let's discuss the second step of the broadcast in the following simple three-GPU setting format, as shown in *Figure 4.5*. It works as follows:

1. **GPU 1** forwards $g\_1 + g\_2 + g\_3$ to **GPU 2** (**forward_1**).
2. **GPU 2** forwards $g\_1 + g\_2 + g\_3$ to **GPU 3** (**forward_2**).

Therefore, for the second step of the broadcast, given N GPUs in use, we need to do N-*1*-*times* forwarding of the aggregated gradients. The time for this N-*1*-*times* forwarding is as follows:

$$t2 = \frac{(N - 1) * g}{BW\_gpu}$$

To summarize, in the All-Reduce architecture, the total time for model synchronization among N nodes is as follows:

$$t\_ar = t1 + t2$$

Key Points to Remember

The time consumption of model synchronization in the All-Reduce architecture is as follows:

Step 1 involves aggregating the gradient time (*t1*):

$$t1 = \frac{N * g}{BW\_gpu}$$

Step 2 involves updating the model time (*t2*):

$$t2 = \frac{(N - 1) * g}{BW\_gpu}$$

So, the total time for model synchronization is as follows:

$$t\_ar = t1 + t2$$

Let's highlight the time consumptions of our two-step All-Reduce architecture:

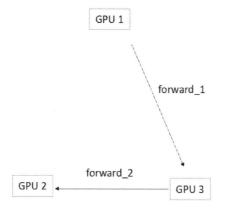

Figure 4.5 – Step-2 broadcast in the All-Reduce architecture

Note that in the *Step-1* Reduce process, the gradient aggregation (for example, **GPU 2** calculating g_1+g_2) on each GPU also takes time. Since the GPU has huge computational power, the time for gradient aggregation is often negligible.

Similar to the *parameter server architecture*, the model synchronization in the *All-Reduce paradigm* also happens after each training iteration. The model synchronization in the All-Reduce paradigm also introduces a huge communication overhead. State-of-the-art literature reports similar model synchronization overhead to the parameter server architecture, which is up to 50% of the end-to-end **deep neural network** (**DNN**) training time. This overhead can be amplified if multiple GPUs/nodes share the same physical link (for example, multiple GPUs share the same PCI-e bus for model synchronization within a machine) due to network congestion.

The inefficiency of state-of-the-art communication schemes

Now, let's talk about the inefficiency that's caused by widely used model synchronization schemes such as **NVIDIA Collective Communication Library** (**NCCL**) from NVIDIA and **Gloo** from Facebook. The most popular solution is NCCL, which is the default communication scheme in PyTorch. Therefore, we will mainly discuss the inefficiency in the NCCL protocol, namely **Ring All-Reduce**.

Let's make the previously discussed three-GPU example a little bit more complicated. Let's assume that we have four GPUs that are fully connected, which is very common in state-of-the-art hardware such as **NVIDIA DGX-1** and **Google TPUs**. The network topology for this four-GPU setting is as follows:

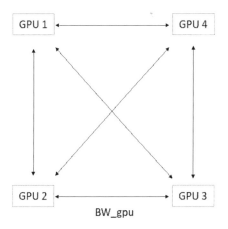

Figure 4.6 – GPU fully connected topology

As shown in the preceding diagram, fully connected means that each GPU has an independent direct link to each of the other GPUs. For example, **GPU 1** has three links. Each link independently connects **GPU 1** to **GPU 2, GPU 3,** and **GPU 4.**

In this four-GPU fully connected setting, if we adopt the Ring All-Reduce scheme, as shown in the following diagram, it will only use the border links (blue links) and make the cross-bar links in the middle (red links) unused:

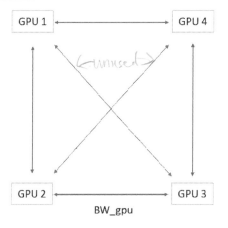

Figure 4.7 – Ring All-Reduce underutilizes two red links in the middle

The reason for the two links in the middle being unused is that these two red links cannot form a new ring topology. The primary assumption of Ring All-Reduce is to first form a network topology into rings. If some links cannot form a ring, Ring All-Reduce simply abandons them.

For scarce resources such as communication links, this *no-ring-no-use* policy is very inefficient. It makes the model's synchronization performance even worse since we directly waste some communication link bandwidth.

Next, we will discuss techniques that achieve higher link utilization.

Leveraging idle links and host resources

In the previous section, we discussed how the communication bottleneck of model synchronization may cause up to 50% of the end-to-end DNN training time. In addition, the widely used NCCL Ring All-Reduce directly abandons some of the scarce communication links if they cannot form a ring.

In this section, we will discuss how we can fully leverage all the communication links within a data parallel training environment. Then, we will discuss how to extend it to using idle links on the host (that is, CPU) side.

Tree All-Reduce

Let's continue using the previous four-GPU fully connected example. As we discussed in the previous section (and as shown in *Figure 4.7*), the two links in the middle are unused, which is a waste of scarce communication resources.

Now, let's introduce a new All-Reduce protocol, which is called Tree All-Reduce. It also works in two steps:

1. First, it sends a portion of the gradients to other nodes.
2. Then, it locally aggregates the received gradients before broadcasting the aggregated gradients to all the other nodes.

This may sound a little bit complicated. Let's continue using the four-GPU example for illustration purposes. As shown in the following diagram, first, we partition the gradients on each node into four chunks – a_i, b_i, c_i, d_i – where i ranges from 1 to 4:

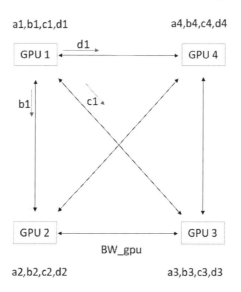

Figure 4.8 – Step-1 communication in Tree All-Reduce for the fully connected setting

During the first step of Tree All-Reduce, the following four things happen concurrently:

- **GPU 1** sends **b1** to **GPU 2**, sends **c1** to **GPU 3**, and sends **d1** to **GPU 4**.
- **GPU 2** sends **a2** to **GPU 1**, sends **c2** to **GPU 3**, and sends **d2** to **GPU 4**.
- **GPU 3** sends **a3** to **GPU 1**, sends **b3** to **GPU 2**, and sends **d3** to **GPU 4**.
- **GPU 4** sends **a4** to **GPU 1**, sends **b4** to **GPU 2**, and sends **c4** to **GPU 3**.

To make the preceding diagram less complicated, we only highlighted the data that's sent from **GPU 1** to all the other GPUs. In practice, four GPUs send separate data chunks to the corresponding GPUs concurrently.

After *Step 1* of communication, the data on each GPU is listed as follows:

- **GPU 1: a1-4, b1, c1, d1**
- **GPU 2: a2, b1-4, c2, d2**
- **GPU 3: a3, b3, c1-4, d3**
- **GPU 4: a4, b4, c4, d1-4**

Then, each GPU will do partial gradient aggregation, as follows:

- **GPU 1**: **A = a1+a2+a3+a4**

- **GPU 2**: **B = b1+b2+b3+b4**

- **GPU 3**: **C = c1+c2+c3+c4**

- **GPU 4**: **D = d1+d2+d3+d4**

After this data aggregation is completed, each GPU will broadcast its aggregated gradients to all the other GPUs, as shown in the following diagram:

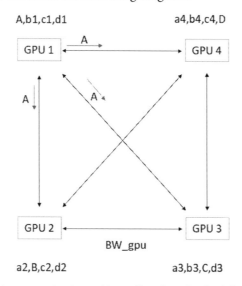

Figure 4.9 – Step-2 communication in Tree All-Reduce for the fully connected setting

As shown in the preceding diagram, *Step 2* of communication conducts the following data transfer simultaneously:

- **GPU 1**: Broadcast **A** to **GPU 2, 3, 4**

- **GPU 2**: Broadcast **B** to **GPU 1, 3, 4**

- **GPU 3**: Broadcast **C** to **GPU 1, 2, 4**

- **GPU 4**: Broadcast **D** to **GPU 1, 2, 3**

After *Step 2* of communication, the model synchronization completes, where each GPU gets all the aggregated gradients of **A**, **B**, **C**, and **D**, as shown in the following diagram:

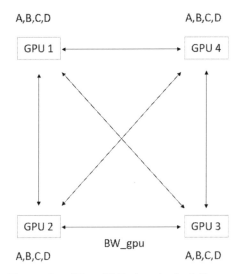

Figure 4.10 – The results of Tree All-Reduce in the fully connected setting

Here, we discussed how Tree All-Reduce works in fully connected settings. Now, let's look at another practical case where GPUs have a different number of communication links.

As shown in the following diagram, this is a four-GPU setting inside an NVIDIA DGX-1 machine:

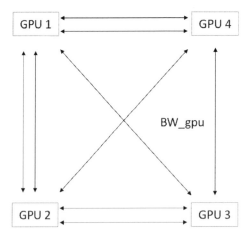

Figure 4.11 – Network topology among four GPUs inside a DGX-1 machine

As shown in the preceding diagram, different GPUs have a different number of links connected to other GPUs. For example, *GPU 1* has five links in total, whereas *GPU 4* has four links in total. We assume each link has the same bandwidth as BW_gpu.

In this asymmetric network topology setting, what Ring All-Reduce does is create two rings, which are denoted as blue and yellow rings (with narrower double-arrow lines) in the following diagram. Then, Ring All-Reduce splits each GPU's gradients in half. They simultaneously communicate the first half of the gradients over one ring and the second half over the other ring:

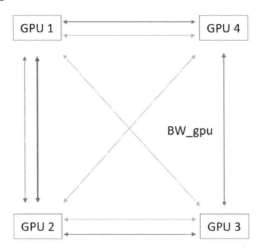

Figure 4.12 – Ring All-Reduce passing the gradients over the blue and yellow rings (the red link remains unused)

More specifically, it works as follows:

- The first half of the gradient passes through the ring: **GPU 1**<->**GPU 2**<->**GPU 3**<->**GPU 4**<->**GPU 1 (blue)**.

- The second half of the gradient passes through the ring: **GPU 1**<->**GPU 4**<->**GPU 2**<->**GPU 3**<->**GPU 1 (yellow)**.

However, as shown in the preceding diagram, one link remains unused, which is denoted by the red (thicker) arrow line. This also indicates that the ring-based solution often underutilizes hardware links. For each GPU, it takes *t_ring* time to finish one round of data forward, where *t_ring* is defined as follows:

$$t\_ring = \frac{g}{2 * BW\_gpu}$$

The reason for having a *2* in the denominator is that we have two rings for the concurrent data transfer process.

On the contrary, Tree All-Reduce can fully utilize all the links in this four-GPU setting, as shown in the following diagram:

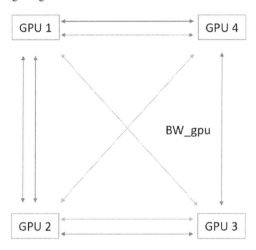

Figure 4.13 – Tree All-Reduce passing the gradients over three trees (no links are wasted)

As shown in the previous diagram, Tree All-Reduce packs three trees together within this network topology. Since we have three concurrent data transfer channels, the time for one round of data forwarding on each GPU is as follows:

$$t\_tree = \frac{g}{3 * BW\_gpu}$$

Here, *t_tree* is smaller than *t_ring*, since we have *3* in the denominator, which is bigger than *2* in the ring case. This simple comparison shows why Tree All-Reduce can achieve faster model synchronization than Ring All-Reduce.

Compared to the tree-based solution we discussed in *Figures 4.8* to *4.10*, Tree All-Reduce is slightly different from the previous fully connected setting. At a high level, it still works in two steps:

1. First, we must pick a root node, where we reduce toward the root node.
2. After aggregating all the gradients, the root node broadcasts its aggregated gradients in the reverse direction of *Step 1*.

Let's look at one tree, which is depicted by the yellow links (the lightest color links) in the preceding diagram. Since we have three trees here, each tree is responsible for 1/3 of the total gradient communication. We pick the root node as *GPU 1*. It works as follows:

Step 1 – Reduce:

1. **GPU 4** sends its 1/3 *g_4* to **GPU2**.
2. **GPU 2** aggregates 1/3 of the gradient as *1/3(g_2 + g_4)*, then passes it to **GPU 3**.
3. **GPU 3** aggregates 1/3 of the gradient as *1/3(g_2 + g_3 + g_4)*, then passes it to **GPU 1**.
4. **GPU 1** finishes aggregating all the 1/3 total gradients (*g_1 + g_2 + g_3 + g_4*) as *1/3G*.

Step 2 – Broadcast:

1. **GPU 1** sends *1/3G to* **GPU 3**
2. **GPU 3** forwards 1/3G to **GPU 2**
3. **GPU 2** forwards 1/3G to **GPU 4**

After these two steps, the Tree All-Reduce on the yellow links is complete. The other two trees work similarly but on different root nodes.

> **Key Points to Remember**
>
> The following points explain how Tree All-Reduce is better than Ring All-Reduce:
>
> (1) Given an arbitrary network topology, the tree-based solution can create more concurrent data transfer channels than the ring-based solution. Therefore, the tree-based solution is faster.
>
> (2) The tree-based solution can leverage more network links than the ring-based solution. Therefore, the tree-based solution is more efficient.

Hybrid data transfer over PCIe and NVLink

So far, we have only discussed using homogenous links for model synchronization. Here, homogenous links refer to links that have the same network bandwidth. In reality, we have multiple kinds of links with different network bandwidths. These are called **heterogeneous network environments**.

One simple example is an NVIDIA DGX-1 machine. Among the GPUs, we have two different kinds of interconnects, as follows:

- **PCIe bus**: A shared link, where the bandwidth is 10 GB/s
- **NVLink**: GPU-exclusive, where the bandwidth is 20-25 GB/s

In a four-GPU setting, the NVlink topology is what was shown in *Figure 4.11*. Let's depict the PCI-e network topology in this four-GPU setting too, as shown here:

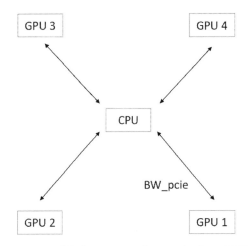

Figure 4.14 – Simplified PCI-e topology in the four-GPU setting

For simplicity, in the preceding diagram, we ignore the PCIe switches and I/O hubs between the GPUs and the CPU. At a high level, the PCIe hierarchy naturally forms a tree structure. Thus, we can directly apply our Tree All-Reduce over the PCIe bus. Therefore, we can use the host idle communication links for our concurrent model synchronization.

In this four-GPU setting, besides the three NVLink trees we created in *Figure 4.13*, here, we are using the PCIe bus to create the fourth tree for All-Reduce. However, since they have different network bandwidths, we need to balance the data transfer between NVLink and PCIe so that they can finish their communication at roughly the same time.

To simplify this load balancing problem, let's assume we have two trees – one PCIe tree and one NVLink tree. We can do network load balancing as follows:

- Calculate the BW ratio: $R = BW\_NVLink / BW\_PCIe$.
- Split the total data into $1+R$ chunks.

- Concurrently transfer the data over PCIe and NVLink. The data size of PCIe should be *1/(1+R)* of the total data, while the data size on NVLink should be *R/(1+R)* of the total data.

By performing the previous three steps, we can enable model synchronization by using heterogeneous hardware links together.

Next, we will discuss another data parallel training bottleneck that is limited to on-device memory.

On-device memory bottlenecks

Nowadays, CPU memory is often tens or hundreds of gigabytes in size. Compared to this huge host of memory, the GPU memory size is often quite limited. The following table shows the commonly used GPU memory sizes:

GPU type	On-device memory size
NVIDIA 1080	8 GB
NVIDIA RTX 2080	8 GB
NVIDIA K80	12 GB
NVIDIA V100	16 GB
NVIDIA A100	40 GB

Figure 4.15 – Different GPU and on-device memory sizes

As shown in the preceding table, even with state-of-the-art GPUs such as the A100, the memory size is only 40 GB. More popular GPU choices, such as the NVIDIA 2080 or K80, only have a GPU memory size of around 10 GB.

When conducting DNN training, those generated intermediate results (for example, feature maps) are often orders of magnitude bigger than the original input data. Thus, it makes the GPU memory limitation more pronounced.

There are mainly two ways to reduce the memory footprint on the accelerators: recomputation and quantization. Let's take a look.

Recomputation and quantization

To reduce the memory footprint during DNN training, we have two main kinds of methodology – **recomputation** and **quantization**.

Recomputation refers to the process where, if some tensors are not used for a certain period, we can delete the tensors and then recompute the result once we need it later.

At a high level, quantization means that we use fewer physical bits to represent a single value. For example, if a normal integer value consumes 4 bytes, by conducting quantization over this integer value, we use 2 bytes or even fewer bits to represent the same value. Quantization is **lossy optimization**, which means it may lose some information while shrinking the bits so that they represent the weights/gradients.

A comparison between these two approaches is illustrated in the following table:

	Recomputation	Quantization
Lossy/lossless	Lossless	Lossy
Reducing memory footprint	Yes	Yes
Computation overhead	Medium	Low

Figure 4.16 – A comparison of the two methods for reducing memory footprints

Recomputation is performed to reproduce the previous results when needed. Thus, it is a lossless computation process. As we mentioned previously, most quantization methods are lossy methods. Both recomputation and quantization can reduce the on-device memory footprint. In addition, compared to recomputation, the computation overhead in quantization is usually much smaller. This is mainly because quantization does not need to go over the computation with DNN layers, which is a computationally heavy workload.

Next, we will cover common techniques that are used in recomputation. Then, we will discuss popular quantization schemes.

Recomputation

Let's assume we have a three-layer DNN, as shown in the following diagram:

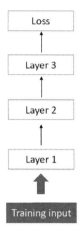

Figure 4.17 – A simple three-layer DNN for recomputation

As we can see, we have a three-layer DNN (layers 1, 2, and 3). Therefore, during forward propagation, we pass training data into the DNN. It will calculate the prediction value. Then, we will calculate the loss as the difference between the predicted values and the target values.

The intermediate results that we need to keep inside forward propagation are shown in the following diagram. The *Activation* (blue) boxes shown on the left-hand side are for forward propagation. For example, *Activation 1* is the intermediate result when we forward propagate training input over layer 1:

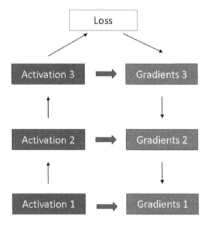

Figure 4.18 – Forward and backward propagation for one training iteration

Backward propagation, labeled as *Gradients* (orange boxes), are shown on the right-hand side in the preceding diagram. After we calculate the loss for the current training batch, we must calculate the gradients on the last layer of the neuron net (that is, **Gradients 3** in the preceding diagram). To calculate **Gradients 3,** we need both the output of the loss function and the previously stored activation values (that is, **Activation 3** in the preceding diagram).

After we calculate **Gradients 3,** we can free the memory that stores **Activation 3.** Similarly, to calculate **Gradients 2,** we need both **Activation 2** and the output of **Gradients 3.** After generating **Gradients 2,** we can release the memory that stores **Activation 2,** and so on.

Based on the preceding analysis, we can see that **Activation 1** is not being used until we calculate **Gradients 1,** which is the last step of backward propagation. With this insight, for **Activation 1,** our recomputation method works as follows:

1. After generating the output of **Activation 1,** we can simply delete it and free the memory.

2. During the backward propagation of generating **Gradients 2,** we can recompute **Activation 1** one more time and store it in memory.

3. Finally, we use both **Activation 1** and the output of **Gradients 2** to calculate **Gradients 1.**

Let's go through the preceding three steps using our previous three-layer DNN example. As shown in the following diagram, by default, **A1** (that is, **Activation 1**) will stay in GPU memory for a long time. **A3** (that is, **Activation 3**) stays for the minimum amount of time, which is the most efficient one regarding memory consumption. The duration of **A2** (that is, **Activation 2**) is in the middle of **A1** and **A3:**

Figure 4.19 – Duration of memory usage for both the activations and gradients

Now, we want to free the memory that's used for storing **A1.** As shown in the following diagram, after we generate the output of **A1** and start computing **A2,** we free the memory that's used for storing **A1.**

During backward propagation, when we generate **G2** (that is, **Gradients 2**), at the same time, we recalculate **A1** using layer 1 and the input data batch. Then, we use the recomputed **A1** and **G2** values to generate **G1** (that is, **Gradients 1**):

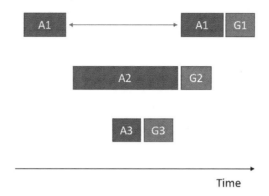

Figure 4.20 – Conducting recomputation on A1 (Activation 1)

By conducting recomputation on **A1**, we can save the memory size of **A1** for the amount of time shown as a double-arrow line in the preceding diagram.

A similar thing can also be applied to **A2**, as shown in the following diagram.

Therefore, by conducting recomputation on this simple three-layer DNN, the amount of GPU memory we can save is as follows:

- Size of **A1** for the same amount of time as **t1** in the following diagram

- Size of **A2** for the same amount of time as **t2** in the following diagram

Note that our example is a very shallow neural network (it only has three layers), so the performance gain can be more significant if we have very deep neural networks (for example, a DNN with hundreds of layers):

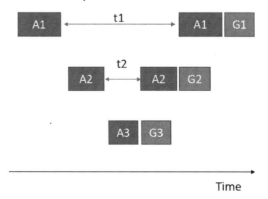

Figure 4.21 – Recomputation on both A1 and A2 (Activation 1 and Activation 2)

So far, we have discussed how to leverage the recomputation method to reduce the memory footprint during DNN training. The overhead that was introduced here was on the computation resources. Basically, for each layer of the neural network, we may need to recompute its activation twice (rather than once) on every training iteration.

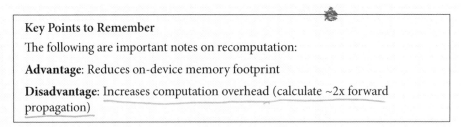

Key Points to Remember

The following are important notes on recomputation:

Advantage: Reduces on-device memory footprint

Disadvantage: Increases computation overhead (calculate ~2x forward propagation)

Next, we will discuss another method for reducing memory footprints. It does not introduce as much computation overhead as recomputation does.

Quantization

Quantization is another common way to reduce memory consumption on the accelerators. The basic idea is pretty simple: use fewer bits to represent the same value.

Right now, a standard representation of an integer needs 4 bytes (32 bits). However, as shown in the following diagram, if you only have integer values of either **0** or **3**, you can just use **1** bit to represent it. As shown at the top of the following diagram, **0** means **0** and **1** means **3**:

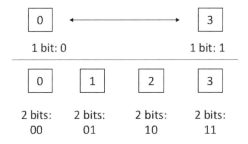

Figure 4.22 – A simple quantization method for representing a value between 0 and 3

If we have four discrete values between **0** and **3** (that is, **0**, **1**, **2**, and **3**), we need to use **2** bits to represent each of the four values. As shown at the bottom of the preceding diagram, **00** means **0**, **01** means **1**, **10** means **2**, and **11** means **3**.

A popular library that's used for model tensor quantization is **Automatic Mixed Precision** (**AMP**), from NVIDIA. To use it, you must simply wrap your optimizer with the function they provide.

Take **TensorFlow** as an example. You can just change the optimizer by using the following code:

```
optimizer = tf.keras.optimizers.SGD()
opt = tf.train.experimental.enable_mixed_precision_graph_
rewrite(optimizer)
```

By adding this `mixed_precision` wrap function on top of your optimizer, NVIDIA will automatically perform quantization on the DNN tensors.

At a high level, what **NVIDIA AMP** does is use a half-precision data format (*FP16*) to represent single-precision values (*TF32*).

One thing worth mentioning is that *FP16* is not used to represent all *TF32* values. Based on the scale and granularity of the values, NVIDIA will automatically determine whether to keep the value in *TF32* format or shrink it down to *FP16* format.

The downside of the quantization method is that it is a lossy data transformation method, which means it loses some information from the original values. For example, with quantization, we may treat both *1* and *1.01* as *1*. Therefore, for *1.01*, we lost the information of *0.01*.

Most of the time, performing quantization, will not cause severe problems in that the model won't converge. However, it is reported that quantization can cause DNN model training to converge to a worse local minimum compared to using a full-precision value representation.

Summary

In this chapter, we discussed two major bottlenecks in the data parallel training process – communication and on-device memory.

Communication becomes a bottleneck during model synchronization. To make things even worse, the Ring All-Reduce solution also wastes some network links that cannot form a ring. Thus, we propose a tree-based All-Reduce solution, which is more efficient and can achieve faster model synchronization than ring-based solutions.

To mitigate the issue of memory, we discussed two major methods – recomputation and quantization.

In the next chapter, we will explore model parallelism, which is another kind of popular paradigm for in-parallel model training and inference. Instead of splitting the input data, model parallelism partitions the model itself.

Section 2 – Model Parallelism

In this section, you will learn about vanilla mode parallelism and pipeline parallelism. You will also implement model-parallel training and an inference pipeline, and learn some further optimization schemes.

This section comprises the following chapters:

- *Chapter 5, Splitting the Model*
- *Chapter 6, Pipeline Input and Layer Split*
- *Chapter 7, Implementing Model Parallel Training and Serving Workflows*
- *Chapter 8, Achieving Higher Throughput and Lower Latency*

5
Splitting the Model

In this chapter, we will discuss how to train giant models with **model parallelism**. **Giant models** refers to models that are too large to fit into a single GPU's memory. Some examples of giant models include **Bidirectional Encoder Representations from Transformers (BERT), Generative Pre-Trainer Transformer (GPT): GPT-2 and GPT-3**.

In contrast to data parallel workloads, model parallelism is often adopted for language models. Language models are a specific type of deep learning model that works in the **Natural Language Processing (NLP)** domain. Here, the input data is usually text sequences. The model outputs predictions for tasks such as question answering and next sentence prediction.

NLP model training is often segregated into two different types, **pre-training** and **fine-tuning**. Pre-training means training the whole giant model from scratch, which may need a huge amount of data and plenty of training epochs. Fine-tuning uses pre-trained models as the base model. We can then fine-tune the base model on some specific downstream tasks. Thus, fine-tuning usually takes much less time to train than pre-training. Also, a fine-tuning dataset is much smaller compared to a pre-training dataset.

Some general assumptions for this chapter are listed as follows:

- For each NLP training job, we usually focus on the fine-tuning process and not the pre-training process.

- For the fine-tuning process, we use a much smaller training dataset than the training data used in the pre-training process.

- We assume each job ran exclusively on a set of GPUs or other accelerators.

- We assume a model has enough layers to split across multiple GPUs.

- We assume we always have a pre-trained model available for fine-tuning.

In this chapter, we will first explain why model parallelism is important by pointing out that single-node training for giant models can cause out-of-memory errors on accelerators. Second, we will briefly discuss several representative NLP models, given that people may not be familiar with these giant models if they have never tried model-parallel training. Third, we will discuss two separate training stages of using pre-trained giant models. Finally, we will explore some state-of-the-art hardware for training these giant models.

In summary, you will learn the following topics in this chapter:

- Single-node training error – out of memory

- ELMo, BERT, and GPT

- Pre-training and fine-tuning

- State-of-the-art hardware

Technical requirements

For the implementation in the rest of the sections, we may illustrate it in BERT or GPT models. We will use the **Stanford Question Answering Dataset (SQuAD 2.0)** as our dataset. We will also use **PyTorch** for illustration. The main library dependencies for our code are as follows:

- torch>=1.7.1

- transformers>=4.10.3

- cuda>=11.0

- NVIDIA driver>=450.119.03

It is mandatory to have the preceding libraries pre-installed with their correct versions.

> **Dataset Citation**
>
> *SQuAD: 100,000+ Questions for Machine Comprehension of Text, Pranav Rajpurkar, Jian Zhang, Konstantin Lopyrev, and Percy Liang, arXiv preprint arXiv:1606.05250* (2016): https://rajpurkar.github.io/SQuAD-explorer/.

Single-node training error – out of memory

Giant NLP models, such as BERT, are often hard to train using a single GPU (that is, single-node). The main reason is due to the limited on-device memory size.

Here, we will first fine-tune the BERT model using a single GPU. The dataset we will use is SQuAD 2.0. It often throws an **Out-of-Memory** (**OOM**) error due to the giant model size and huge intermediate results size.

Second, we will use a state-of-the-art GPU and try our best to pack the relatively small BERT-base model inside a single GPU. Then, we will carefully adjust the batch size to avoid an OOM error.

Fine-tuning BERT on a single GPU

The first thing we need to do is to install the transformers library on our machine. Here, we use the transformers library provided by **Hugging Face**. The following command is how we install it on an Ubuntu machine using PyTorch:

```
$ pip install transformers
```

Please make sure you are installing the correct transformers version (>=4.10.3) by double-checking, as follows:

```
Python 3.7.10 | packaged by conda-forge | (default, Feb 19 2021, 16:07:37)
[GCC 9.3.0] on linux
Type "help", "copyright", "credits" or "license" for more information.
>>> import transformers
>>> print(transformers.__version__)
4.10.3
>>>
```

Figure 5.1 – Checking the transformers version

Then, we can start using the pre-trained model for our fine-tuning tasks.

We will illustrate how to implement the training process in the later sections. Now, assuming we have successfully started the training job, it prints out the following error messages:

```
Training epoch  1
  0%|                                                                          | 0/86136
[00:00<?, ?it/s]Traceback (most recent call last):
  File "bert.py", line 198, in <module>
    end_positions=end_token_idx, return_dict=False)
  File "/home/ubuntu/anaconda3/envs/pytorch_latest_p37/lib/python3.7/site-packages/torch/nn/modules/module.py",
line 889, in _call_impl
    result = self.forward(*input, **kwargs)
  File "/home/ubuntu/anaconda3/envs/pytorch_latest_p37/lib/python3.7/site-packages/transformers/models/bert/mode
ling_bert.py", line 1825, in forward
    return_dict=return_dict,
  File "/home/ubuntu/anaconda3/envs/pytorch_latest_p37/lib/python3.7/site-packages/torch/nn/modules/module.py",
line 889, in _call_impl
    result = self.forward(*input, **kwargs)
  File "/home/ubuntu/anaconda3/envs/pytorch_latest_p37/lib/python3.7/site-packages/transformers/models/bert/mode
ling_bert.py", line 1000, in forward
    return_dict=return_dict,
  File "/home/ubuntu/anaconda3/envs/pytorch_latest_p37/lib/python3.7/site-packages/torch/nn/modules/module.py",
line 889, in _call_impl
    result = self.forward(*input, **kwargs)
  File "/home/ubuntu/anaconda3/envs/pytorch_latest_p37/lib/python3.7/site-packages/transformers/models/bert/mode
ling_bert.py", line 589, in forward
    output_attentions,
  File "/home/ubuntu/anaconda3/envs/pytorch_latest_p37/lib/python3.7/site-packages/torch/nn/modules/module.py",
line 889, in _call_impl
    result = self.forward(*input, **kwargs)
  File "/home/ubuntu/anaconda3/envs/pytorch_latest_p37/lib/python3.7/site-packages/transformers/models/bert/mode
ling_bert.py", line 511, in forward
    self.feed_forward_chunk, self.chunk_size_feed_forward, self.seq_len_dim, attention_output
  File "/home/ubuntu/anaconda3/envs/pytorch_latest_p37/lib/python3.7/site-packages/transformers/modeling_utils.p
y", line 2196, in apply_chunking_to_forward
    return forward_fn(*input_tensors)
  File "/home/ubuntu/anaconda3/envs/pytorch_latest_p37/lib/python3.7/site-packages/transformers/models/bert/mode
ling_bert.py", line 522, in feed_forward_chunk
    intermediate_output = self.intermediate(attention_output)
  File "/home/ubuntu/anaconda3/envs/pytorch_latest_p37/lib/python3.7/site-packages/torch/nn/modules/module.py",
line 889, in _call_impl
    result = self.forward(*input, **kwargs)
  File "/home/ubuntu/anaconda3/envs/pytorch_latest_p37/lib/python3.7/site-packages/transformers/models/bert/mode
ling_bert.py", line 426, in forward
    hidden_states = self.intermediate_act_fn(hidden_states)
  File "/home/ubuntu/anaconda3/envs/pytorch_latest_p37/lib/python3.7/site-packages/torch/nn/functional.py", line
1459, in gelu
    return torch._C._nn.gelu(input)
RuntimeError: CUDA out of memory. Tried to allocate 144.00 MiB (GPU 0; 15.78 GiB total capacity; 14.19 GiB alrea
dy allocated; 102.75 MiB free; 14.25 GiB reserved in total by PyTorch)
  0%|                                                                          | 0/86136
[00:04<?, ?it/s]
```

Figure 5.2 – Error messages

The preceding error messages indicate that the training job has run OOM on the GPUs. It indicates that a single GPU is not enough for holding a giant model and gives some intermediate results from the inputs.

A Single GPU Training Giant NLP Models

Using a single GPU to train a giant NLP model will cause an OOM error. The main reason for this is that the model parameter size is too large. Consequently, the intermediate results generated from the input are also very large.

Given this OOM error, it is natural to think about splitting the model and spreading the model partitions across different GPUs. This is what we call model parallelism.

Model Parallelism

Model parallelism works by taking the following two steps:

1. Splitting the model weights into a disjoint subset

2. Spreading each model partition onto a single accelerator

Before we dive into model parallelism, we will first try to use one state-of-the-art GPU, **NVIDIA V100**, to pack a relatively small BERT model into a single GPU. We will discuss the pros and cons of doing this in the following section.

Trying to pack a giant model inside one state-of-the-art GPU

Here, we will try to use a state-of-the-art GPU, which is NVIDIA V100. The following figure shows the technical specifications of a V100 GPU:

```
Mon Sep 27 19:40:34 2021
+-----------------------------------------------------------------------------+
| NVIDIA-SMI 450.119.03   Driver Version: 450.119.03   CUDA Version: 11.0     |
|-------------------------------+----------------------+----------------------+
| GPU  Name        Persistence-M| Bus-Id        Disp.A | Volatile Uncorr. ECC |
| Fan  Temp  Perf  Pwr:Usage/Cap|         Memory-Usage | GPU-Util  Compute M. |
|                               |                      |               MIG M. |
|===============================+======================+======================|
|   0  Tesla V100-SXM2...  On   | 00000000:00:1E.0 Off |                    0 |
| N/A   35C    P0    23W / 300W |      0MiB / 16160MiB |      0%      Default |
|                               |                      |                  N/A |
+-------------------------------+----------------------+----------------------+

+-----------------------------------------------------------------------------+
| Processes:                                                                  |
|  GPU   GI   CI        PID   Type   Process name                  GPU Memory |
|        ID   ID                                                   Usage      |
|=============================================================================|
|  No running processes found                                                 |
+-----------------------------------------------------------------------------+
```

Figure 5.3 – Technical specifications of a V100 GPU

As shown in the preceding figure, a V100 GPU has `16160MiB` (~16 GB) of on-device memory. The peak power consumption can be `300W`. This is one of the GPUs that has the largest on-device memory size.

Now, let's try to pack a BERT-base model into this single V100 GPU.

Before the training starts, we need to preprocess the input data, which is as follows:

```
Creating training points: 100%|          | 442/442 [01:20<00:00,  5.47it/s]
Creating evaluation points: 100%|          | 48/48 [00:09<00:00,  4.98it/s]
86136 training points created.
10331 evaluation points created.
```

Figure 5.4 – Preprocessing the input data

After we generate the training samples, we launch our training job.

To fit into a single GPU's memory, here we use a very small batch size of four. The following is the system information on fine-tuning BERT with the SQuAD 2.0 dataset:

```
+-----------------------------------------------------------------------------+
| NVIDIA-SMI 450.119.03   Driver Version: 450.119.03   CUDA Version: 11.0     |
|-------------------------------+----------------------+----------------------+
| GPU  Name        Persistence-M| Bus-Id        Disp.A | Volatile Uncorr. ECC |
| Fan  Temp  Perf  Pwr:Usage/Cap|         Memory-Usage | GPU-Util  Compute M. |
|                               |                      |               MIG M. |
|===============================+======================+======================|
|   0  Tesla V100-SXM2...  On   | 00000000:00:1E.0 Off |                    0 |
| N/A   47C    P0   240W / 300W |   5361MiB / 16160MiB |     83%      Default |
|                               |                      |                  N/A |
+-------------------------------+----------------------+----------------------+

+-----------------------------------------------------------------------------+
| Processes:                                                                  |
|  GPU   GI   CI        PID   Type   Process name                  GPU Memory |
|        ID   ID                                                   Usage      |
|=============================================================================|
|    0   N/A  N/A     13322      C   python                           5359MiB |
+-----------------------------------------------------------------------------+
```

Figure 5.5 – System information on fine-tuning BERT with the SQuAD 2.0 dataset

As shown in the preceding figure, with a batch size of four, the BERT-based model can be trained inside a single V100 GPU. However, when you look at the computation core utility rate (that is, **Volatile GPU-Util** in the preceding figure), it is just around `83%`. This means around 17% of computation cores are wasted.

Note that this volatile GPU-Util rate is a coarse metric, which means that the real GPU core usage is usually even lower than the number that is shown here.

We will also test another extreme case with a batch size of one. The following is the GPU utility status:

```
+-----------------------------------------------------------------------------+
| NVIDIA-SMI 450.119.03   Driver Version: 450.119.03   CUDA Version: 11.0     |
|-------------------------------+----------------------+----------------------+
| GPU  Name        Persistence-M| Bus-Id        Disp.A | Volatile Uncorr. ECC |
| Fan  Temp  Perf  Pwr:Usage/Cap|         Memory-Usage | GPU-Util  Compute M. |
|                               |                      |               MIG M. |
|===============================+======================+======================|
|   0  Tesla V100-SXM2...  On   | 00000000:00:1E.0 Off |                    0 |
| N/A   57C    P0   118W / 300W |   3727MiB / 16160MiB |     65%      Default |
|                               |                      |                  N/A |
+-------------------------------+----------------------+----------------------+

+-----------------------------------------------------------------------------+
| Processes:                                                                  |
|  GPU   GI   CI        PID   Type   Process name                  GPU Memory |
|        ID   ID                                                   Usage      |
|=============================================================================|
|    0   N/A  N/A     14498      C   python                           3725MiB |
+-----------------------------------------------------------------------------+
```

Figure 5.6 – Testing with the batch size as one – GPU utility status

As shown in the preceding figure, the GPU utility in this case is just 65%, which means almost half of the GPU core is wasted during training. One thing worth mentioning is that the training time can be insanely long if we just use a tiny batch size such as one or four.

Another thing is, right now, we only test relatively small models as BERT-base. With some other bigger models, such as BERT-large, GPT-3 is not possible to fit into a single GPU's memory.

To sum up, single-node training often causes an OOM error when training giant NLP models.

Even in some extreme cases, we can pack a relatively small NLP model inside a single GPU. However, it may not be practical due to the following reasons:

- Local training batch size is too small; thus the overall training time will be insanely long.

- A small batch size also leads to the wastage of computation cores.

Next, we will discuss common NLP models used nowadays.

ELMo, BERT, and GPT

In this section, we will explain several classic NLP models used nowadays, namely ELMo, BERT, and GPT.

Before we dive into these complicated model structures, we will first illustrate the basic concept of a **Recurrent Neural Network** (**RNN**) and how it works. Then, we will move on to the transformers. This section will cover the following topics:

- Basic concepts
- RNN
- ELMo
- BERT
- GPT

We will start with introducing RNNs.

Basic concepts

Here, we will dive into the world of RNNs. At a high-level, different from CNNs, an RNN usually needs to maintain the states from previous input. It is just like memory for human beings.

We will illustrate what we mean with the following examples:

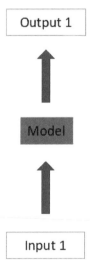

Figure 5.7 – One-to-one problems

As shown in the preceding figure, one-to-one is a typical problem format in the computer vision domain. Basically, assuming we have a CNN model, we input an image as **Input 1**, as shown in *Figure 5.7*. The CNN model will output a prediction value (for example, an image label) as **Output 1** in *Figure 5.7*. This is what we call *one-to-one problems*.

Next, we will discuss one-to-many problems, as illustrated in *Figure 5.8*:

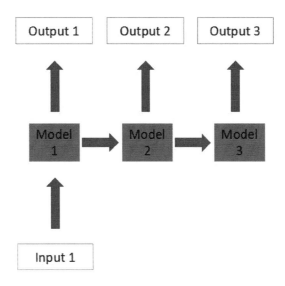

Figure 5.8 – One-to-many problems

What's shown in the preceding figure is another typical task, called a one-to-many problem. It is one of several common tasks for an NLP model, for example, image captioning. We can input an image and the model produces the output as a sentence describing what is inside the image.

It is worth mentioning that models 1, 2, and 3 are the same models as in *Figure 5.8*. The only difference is that **Model 2** received some states information from **Model 1**, and **Model 3** received some states memory from **Model 2**.

Next, we will discuss many-to-one problems, as shown in the following figure:

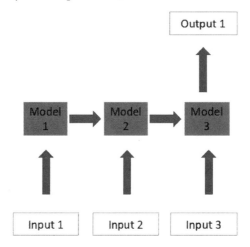

Figure 5.9 – Many-to-one problems

There is another kind of workload that requires an RNN-based model. It is called a many-to-one problem.

Basically, we are given a sequence of inputs (for example, a sentence with multiple words). After processing each word in a sequential order, we output one value. One example of a many-to-one problem would be **sentiment classification**. For example, after reading a sentence from a customer review, the model predicts whether it is a positive comment or a negative one.

Next is a **many-to-many problem**. We have two sub-categories in this setting, which are shown in *Figure 5.10* and *Figure 5.11* respectively:

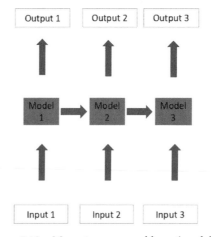

Figure 5.10 – Many-to-many problems (no delay)

The first type of many-to-many problem is the **no-delay version**. This means that, after getting one input, the model will immediately predict one output. As shown in the preceding figure, there is no delay between **Input 1** and **Output 1**, or **Input 2** and **Output 2**.

A common application is video classification and motion capturing. Basically, for each frame of the input image, we need to tag the objects in the picture and monitor their movements.

Next, we will discuss another many-to-many problem with delay, as shown in the following figure:

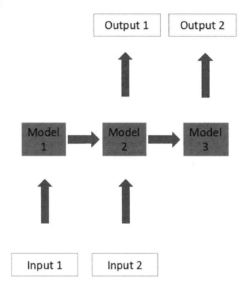

Figure 5.11 – Many-to-many problems (with delay)

As shown in the preceding figure, the second version of a many-to-many problem is having a delay between the input and output. As shown in the preceding figure, **Output 1** will not be generated until we pass in **Input 2**. This is the reason we call it a many-to-many problem with delay.

One typical example of this is machine translation. Basically, once we get the first word of a sentence from language A, we wait and collect more words from the input sentence, and then we provide the output as the translation of the sentence from language A to language B.

RNN

Apart from the one-to-one problem defined in the preceding section, all other problems have some dependency on previous states. For example, in *Figure 5.11*, in order to get **Model 2** weights, we need **Model 1** to memorize some information from **Input 1** and pass this information to **Model 2**.

Although **Model 1** and **Model 2** are the same models, they maintain different intermediate states. For example, in *Figure 5.11*, **Model 2**'s state maintains information from both **Model 1** and **Input 2**.

To pass state information within the same model, we define some recurrent links on the model. A model with a recurrent link is called an RNN, shown in the following figure:

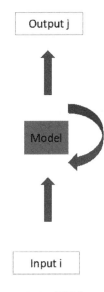

Figure 5.12 – RNN structure

As shown in the preceding figure, the main difference between an RNN and other models such as a CNN is that an RNN has a recurrent link within the model itself.

This recurrent link is used for maintaining input-related states inside the model. For example, when the model receives the second input, it can use both the first input's states and the second input to predict the output.

An unrolled version of an RNN is shown in the following figure. Here, we unroll the RNN in the time dimension:

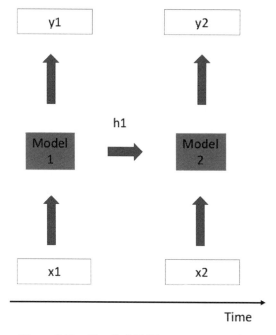

Figure 5.13 – Unrolled RNN structure over time

As shown in the preceding figure, at the first time slot, after the model processes *input 1* (that is, **x1**), it will generate *output 1* (that is, **y1**). At the same time, it will maintain some hidden states (for example, **h1** stands for *hidden state* at *time 1*).

At the second time slot, the model will receive *input 2*. Here, the model will do two things, as follows:

1. Calculate the new hidden state, as follows:

$$h2 \ = \ Wh \ * \ h1 \ + \ Wx \ * \ x2 \ + \ bias$$

Here, *Wh* is the model's weight for memorizing hidden information such as *h1, h2 … ht*. *Wx* is the weight matrix for current input, such as *x2, x3, … xt*. For most DNN models, we also need to add bias at the very end of the calculation.

Basically, to calculate the new hidden state *h2*, we need to aggregate the previous hidden state and current input data.

2. Use the new hidden state *h2* and *x2* to generate the output *y2*, as follows:

$$y2 = Wy * h2 + bias$$

To calculate the output at time slot 2 (that is, **y2** in *Figure 5.13*), we need to use the updated hidden state *h2* and weight matrix for output (that is, *Wy*). Similarly, we add the bias item at the end of this equation.

With the preceding two equations, at any given time *i* we can do the following:

1. Update the hidden state *h[i]* with the previous hidden state *h[i-1]* and current input *x[i]*.

2. Then, use the updated *h[i]* to generate the current output *y[i]*.

These are the key concepts regarding the simplest NLP model, which is an RNN. In a real-world application, we usually stack an RNN as shown in the following figure:

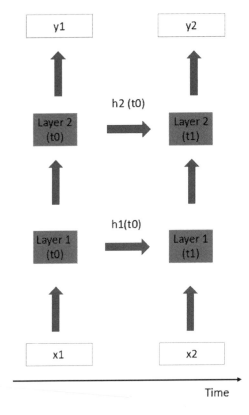

Figure 5.14 – Stacked RNN (deep RNN)

In the preceding figure, we illustrate a simplified stacked RNN that stacks two RNNs together.

You may regard **Layer 1** as the RNN we described in *Figure 5.13*. On top of that, we stack another RNN called **Layer 2**.

Basically, for one particular layer of the stacked RNN, the following applies:

- It takes the previous RNN layer's output as its own input.
- After generating its own output, it passes the output to its successive RNN layer as the input.

It is common that a stacked RNN has a better test accuracy compared with a single-layer RNN. Thus, for a real-world application, a stacked RNN is often a better choice.

ELMo

ELMo is a special kind of RNN. It is based on **Long Short-Term Memory (LSTM)**.

LSTM can be regarded as a complicated version of the RNN we mentioned in the previous section. Basically, each LSTM cell has a multiple-gating system for maintaining both long-term and short-term memory of the data.

In a traditional RNN, the hidden state is always propagated in the same order as the input sequence. In the following figure, for **Layer 1**, the hidden state is passed as **h1_1** and then **h1_2**, which is the same order as inputs **x1** and **x2**:

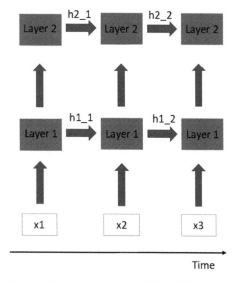

Figure 5.15 – Forward part of the ELMo model

In contrast to a traditional RNN model, ELMo actually maintains another model that backward-propagates hidden states, as seen in the following figure:

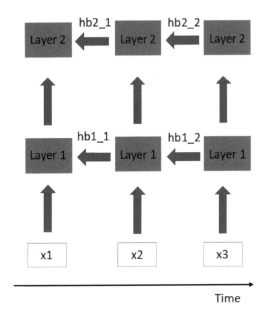

Figure 5.16 – Backward part of the ELMo model

As shown in the preceding figure, ELMo maintains one additional model that backward-propagates the hidden states information. For example, for **Layer 1**, the hidden state is propagated from **hb1_2** to **hb1_1**, which is the inverse order of **x1**, **x2**, and **x3**.

Since ELMo maintains two model parts, one forward-propagates the hidden states and the other backward-propagates the hidden states. Thus, for each input, for a layer, we may have two different hidden states.

For example, in *Figure 5.15* and *Figure 5.16*, for **x2 Layer 1** has a forward hidden state as **h1_1** and a backward hidden state as **hb1_2**. ELMo will use both hidden states to represent **x2**.

Therefore, in ELMo, for a particular input, we have two groups of hidden states, one a group of forward hidden states and the other a group of backward hidden states. This decent feature guarantees that ELMo can learn the input relationship in both forward and backward directions. This richer information contributes to the higher test accuracy of ELMo when comparing with forward-only RNN models.

We have just discussed all the classical models using an RNN. Next, we will discuss transformer-based models, such as BERT and GPT-2/3.

BERT

The **BERT** model was invented by Google. The base component of the BERT model is the **transformer**.

A transformer adopts a similar idea to ELMo's bidirectional training. However, a transformer extends it one step further by adopting self-attention. A **simplified self-attention unit** is shown in the following figure:

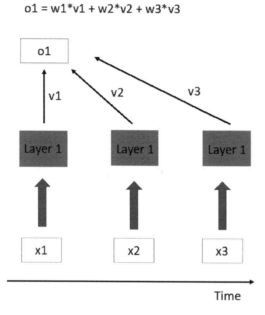

Figure 5.17 – Simplified self-attention

We use the same example as *Figure 5.12*. Let's assume we have a single-layer model, and we want to calculate the output **o1** given the input **x1**. In a self-attention scheme, it removes the direct hidden state, passing links as **h1_1** or **hb1_1** as we saw in *Figure 5.15* and *Figure 5.16* respectively. Instead, self-attention uses all the memory information from all the input tokens (for example, **x1**, **x2**, and **x3** in *Figure 5.17*) together.

For example, in order to calculate **o1** in *Figure 5.17*, self-attention defines the correlation of **x1** with all input tokens (that is, **x1**, **x2**, and **x3**). It works in two steps:

1.   We regard the correlation as a weight matrix, such as **w1**, **w2**, and **w3** in *Figure 5.17*.

2.   Then, we use both correlation matrices and some values generated from each input (that is, **v1**, **v2**, and **v3**) together to calculate output **o1**.

The formal definition for calculating *o1* is as follows:

$$o1 = w1 * v1 + w2 * v2 + w3 * v3$$

For other output such as *o2* and *o3*, it follows the preceding equation as well.

At a high level, the main difference between a bidirectional RNN and self-attention is as follows:

- In a bidirectional RNN (such as ELMo), the hidden state for one input token only depends on its previous or successive input states.

- In self-attention, the intermediate representation of one input token depends on all the input tokens together.

In reality, a transformer uses multi-head attention, which is to calculate multiple attention output values for each input.

For example, for the *o1* case mentioned previously, multi-head attention will calculate *o1_1*, *o1_2*, and so on. Each *o1_i* has different correlation matrices such as *w1_i*, *w2_i*, *w3_i*, and so on.

BERT borrows the bidirectional transformer concepts and stacks multiple layers of bidirectional transformers together, as shown in the following figure:

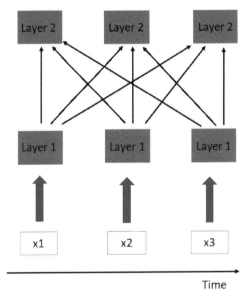

Figure 5.18 – A simplified BERT model

The preceding figure shows a simplified BERT model illustration. We stack two bidirectional transformer layers. Here, a **bidirectional transformer** refers to the attention values for each input that not only depend on all its previous input tokens but also its successive input tokens.

Next, we will discuss GPT, a slightly different transformer-based NLP model.

GPT

A **GPT** model was developed by *OpenAI*, which is also a transformer-based NLP model. Currently, the most popular types of GPT models are GPT-2 and GPT-3. Both GPT-2 and GPT-3 are giant models. The commonly used model versions are not able to fit into a single GPU's memory.

Compared with BERT, GPT models adopt a slightly different transformer as the base components. A simplified structure for a GPT model is shown here:

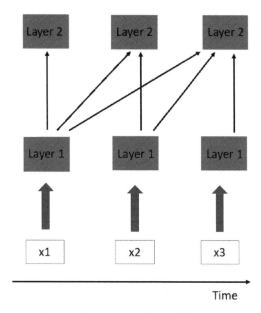

Figure 5.19 – A simplified GPT model

As shown in the preceding figure, the transformer layer here is slightly different than the one in *Figure 5.18*.

Here, each input's attention value only depends on its previous input tokens and is not related to its successive input tokens. Thus, we call it a **one-directional transformer** or **forward-only transformer**, while we call the BERT-version transformer shown in *Figure 5.18* a bidirectional transformer.

Next, we will discuss two types of NLP model training.

Pre-training and fine-tuning

There are two stages in NLP models that can be described as training. One is pre-training and the other is fine-tuning. In this section, we will discuss the main difference between these two concepts.

Pre-training is where we train a giant NLP model from scratch. In pre-training, we need to have a huge training dataset (for example, all the Wikipedia pages). It works as follows:

1. We initialize the model weights.
2. We partition the giant model into hundreds or thousands of GPUs via model parallelism.
3. We feed the huge training dataset into the model-parallel training pipeline and train for several weeks or months.
4. Once the model is converged to a good local minimum, we stop the training and call the model a pre-trained model.

By following the preceding steps, we can get a pre-trained NLP model.

Note that the pre-training process often takes huge amounts of computational resources and time. As of now, only big companies such as *Google* and *Microsoft* have the resources to pre-train a model. Pre-training is rarely seen in academia.

Fine-tuning is to slightly adjust the pre-trained model with different downstream tasks. For example, a BERT model is pre-trained for tasks such as the following:

-   **Masked language modeling**
-   **Next sentence prediction**

However, you can also use BERT for other tasks, such as the following:

-   **Question answering**
-   **Sequence classification**

You need to fine-tune the pre-trained BERT model for these new downstream tasks.

Suppose you train the pre-trained BERT model for question answering. You need to fine-tune the pre-trained BERT model on a much smaller question-answering dataset, such as SQuAD 2.0.

One thing worth mentioning is that, compared to pre-training, the fine-tuning process often takes much less computational resources and costs less training time. In addition, fine-tuning is often training the pre-trained model on some small datasets.

> **Pre-Training versus Fine-Tuning**
>
> Pre-training is when you train a model from scratch.
>
> Fine-tuning is when you adjust the pre-trained model weights with new downstream tasks.

Since most of the NLP models are giant, we often use the best GPUs to train these models concurrently. Next, we will discuss state-of-the-art hardware. We will mainly focus on discussing the GPUs from NVIDIA.

State-of-the-art hardware

Due to the huge computation power needed for training giant NLP models, we usually use a state-of-the-art hardware accelerator to do the NLP model training. In the following sections, we will look into some of the best GPUs and hardware links from NVIDIA.

P100, V100, and DGX-1

Tesla P100 GPU and **Volta V100 GPU** are the best GPUs launched by NVIDIA. Each P100/V100 GPU has the following:

- 5–8 teraflops of double-precision computation power
- 16 GB on-device memory
- 700 GB/s high bandwidth memory I/O
- NVLink-optimized

As per the specification listed in the preceding list, each P100/V100 GPU has a huge amount of computation power. There is an even more powerful machine that includes eight P100/V100 GPUs inside a single box. The eight-P100/V100-GPU box is called **DGX-1**.

DGX-1 is designed for high-performance computation. When embedding eight P100/V100 GPUs inside a single box, the cross-GPU network bandwidth becomes the main bottleneck during in-parallel model training.

Therefore, DGX-1 introduces a new hardware link called **NVLink**.

NVLink

NVLink is a GPU-exclusive, point-to-point communication link among GPUs inside one DGX-1 box.

NVLink can be regarded as a much faster PCIe bus but only connects with GPUs. PCIe 3.0 communication bandwidth is around 10 GB/s. Compared with PCIe, each NVLink can provide around 20–25 GB/s of communication bandwidth among GPUs.

In addition, for the P100 version, the NVLink among the GPUs within a DGX-1 machine forms a special hyper-cube topology, which is shown in *Figure 5.20*.

As shown in *Figure 5.20*, we have two different four-GPU islands. *G0–G3* forms one island and *G4–G7* forms another island. The hyper-cube topology has the following attributes:

- Within one island, the four GPUs are fully connected.

- Between two islands, only counterpart GPUs are connected (for example, *G0–G4* and *G2–G6*).

The following figure shows the hyper-cube topology:

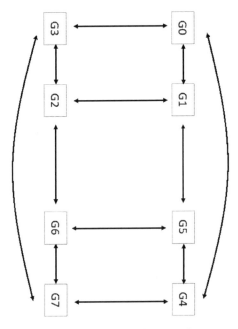

Figure 5.20 – Hyper-cube NVLink topology inside a DGX-1 machine

For DGX-1 with eight V100 GPUs, the NVLink topology looks similar to the preceding figure. More specifically, besides the hyper-cube topology in *Figure 5.20*, DGX-1 (with V100) adds an additional NVLink ring that connects **G0**, **G3**, **G2**, **G6**, **G7**, **G4**, **G5**, and **G1**.

A100 and DGX-2

Currently, the best GPU from NVIDIA is called **A100**. The following are some of the main specifications of A100:

- 10 teraflops of double-precision computation power
- 40 GB on-device memory
- 1,500 GB/s memory bandwidth
- NVSwitch-optimized

The DGX-2 machine packs 16 A100 GPUs inside a single box. These 16 A100s are connected by NVSwitch.

NVSwitch

NVSwitch is the new generation of cross-GPU communication channels. It can be regarded as a switch in computer networks that enables point-to-point communication bandwidth of 150 GB/s unidirectionally and 300 GB/s bidirectionally among GPUs.

Summary

In this chapter, we mainly discussed NLP models and state-of-the-art hardware accelerators. After reading this chapter, you now understand why NLP models are usually not suitable to be trained on a single GPU. You also now know basic concepts such as the structure of an RNN model, a stacked RNN model, ELMo, BERT, and GPT.

Regarding hardware, you now know about several state-of-the-art GPUs from NVIDIA and the high-bandwidth links in between.

In the next chapter, we will cover the details of model parallelism and some techniques to improve system efficiency.

6
Pipeline Input and Layer Split

In this chapter, we will continue our discussion about **model parallelism**. Compared to data parallelism, model parallelism training often takes more GPUs/accelerators. Thus, system efficiency plays an important role during model parallelism training and inference.

We limit our discussion with the following assumptions:

- We assume the input data batches are the same size.

- In **multi-layer perceptrons** (**MLPs**), we assume they can be calculated with **general matrix multiply** (**GEMM**) functions.

- For each NLP job, we run it exclusively over a set of accelerators (for example, GPUs). This means there is no interference from other jobs.

- For each NLP job, we use the same type of accelerator (for example, GPUs).

- GPUs within a machine are connected with homogeneous links (for example, NVLink or PCIe).

- For cross-machine communication, the machines are also connected with homogeneous links (for example, an Ethernet cable).

- For model parallelism training, we are focusing on fine-tuning. Thus, we assume we have a pre-trained NLP model.

- For each input batch, the number of items is large enough to be split into multiple partitions.

- For each layer of the model, there are enough neurons for us to split and re-distribute them to multiple accelerators.

- For the number of layers of an NLP model, there are enough layers for us to partition them among multiple accelerators.

In this chapter, we will mainly focus on system efficiency in model parallelism. First, we will discuss the shortcomings of **vanilla model parallelism**. Vanilla model parallelism cannot scale well mainly due to system inefficiency. Second, we will cover the first kind of approach (pipeline parallelism) to improve system efficiency in model parallelism training. Third, we then describe pipeline parallelism on top of model parallelism in order to improve system efficiency. Fourth, we will discuss the advantages and disadvantages of using pipeline parallelism. Fifth, we will discuss a second kind of approach, that is, intra-layer model parallelism. And lastly, we will discuss variations of intra-layer model parallelism.

In summary, we will cover the following topics in this chapter:

- Vanilla model parallelism is inefficient

- Pipeline parallelism

- Pros and cons of pipeline parallelism

- Layer split

- Notes on intra-layer model parallelism

Now we will illustrate why vanilla model parallelism is very inefficient. Then we will discuss pipeline parallelism and intra-layer model parallelism separately.

Vanilla model parallelism is inefficient

As mentioned in a huge number of papers from academia and technical reports from the industry, vanilla model parallelism is very inefficient regarding GPU computation and memory utilization. To illustrate why vanilla model parallelism is not efficient, let's look at a simple DNN model, which is shown in *Figure 6.1*:

Figure 6.1 – A simple NLP model with three layers

As shown in *Figure 6.1*, given the training input, we pass it into our three-layer NLP model. The layers are denoted as **Layer 1**, **Layer 2**, and **Layer 3**. After the forward propagation, the model will generate some output.

Now let's assume we use three GPUs. Each GPU only holds one layer of the original model. It is shown in *Figure 6.2*:

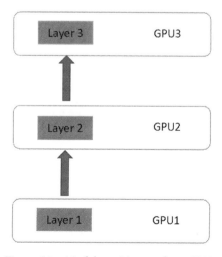

Figure 6.2 – Model partition on three GPUs

In *Figure 6.2*, we have **GPU1** holding **Layer 1** of the model. Similarly, we have **GPU2** holding **Layer 2** and **GPU3** holding **Layer 3**.

Now, we will discuss forward propagation and backward propagation step by step.

Forward propagation

Given a batch of input training data, we will first conduct forward propagation on the model. Since we partition the model onto GPUs 1-3, the forward propagation happens in the following order:

1. **GPU1** will first conduct forward propagation of **Layer 1** on input data.

2. Then, **GPU2** will start forward propagation.

3. Finally, **GPU3** will start forward propagation.

The preceding three-step forward propagation can be visualized as follows:

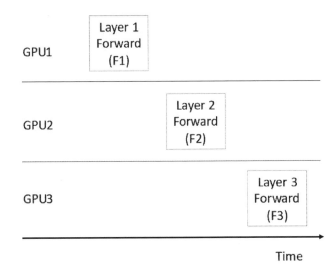

Figure 6.3 – Forward propagation in model parallelism

As shown in *Figure 6.3*, on **GPU1** we conduct Layer 1's forward propagation, and we rename it **F1**. Similarly, **Layer 2**'s forward propagation is called **F2** and **Layer 3**'s forward propagation is called **F3**.

After Layer 3 is finished with forward propagation, it will generate the model's output. The model serving stage is the end of model serving for the current input data batch. However, if you are doing model training (that is, the fine-tuning stage of NLP model training), we need to generate gradients for each layer via backward propagation.

Backward propagation

After Layer 3's forward propagation (that is, **F3** in *Figure 6.3*), it generates an output prediction. At the model parallel training stage, we compare the prediction with the correct label/output via the loss function. Then we start the backward propagation, which is illustrated in the following diagram:

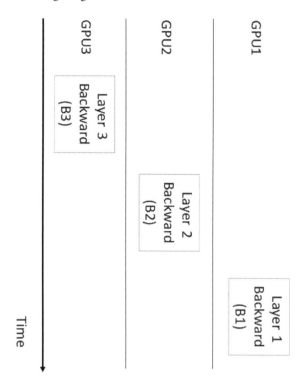

Figure 6.4 – Backward propagation in model parallelism training

As shown in the preceding diagram, compared to forward propagation in *Figure 6.3*, backward propagation is in the reverse order. It works as follows:

1. First, **Layer 3** on **GPU3** starts backward propagation to generate local gradients of **Layer 3.** We call this **Layer 3** backward propagation **B3** in the preceding diagram. Then, **GPU3** will pass **Layer 3'**s gradient output to **Layer 2** on **GPU2**.

2. After receiving **GPU3'**s gradient output, **GPU2** will use it (together with the activations generated from the previous forward propagation) to generate **Layer 2'**s local gradients. We call **Layer 2'**s backward propagation **B2** in *Figure 6.4*. Then, **GPU2** will pass its gradient output to **GPU1**.

3. Finally, **Layer 1** on **GPU1** conducts backward propagation and generates local gradients. We call this step **B1** in *Figure 6.4*.

After all the layers generate their local gradients, we use these gradients to update the model parameters.

In this section, we described the details of forward propagation and backward propagation in model parallelism training. Next, we will analyze the system inefficiency during each training iteration, which consists of one forward propagation and one backward propagation.

GPU idle time between forward and backward propagation

Now let's analyze a whole training iteration, which consists of one forward propagation followed by one backward propagation. We will illustrate it using the previous three-layer model training example.

The whole workflow of one training iteration is depicted in the following diagram:

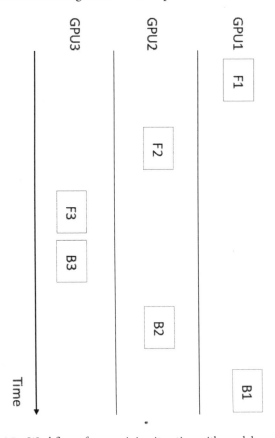

Figure 6.5 – Workflow of one training iteration with model parallelism

The whole workflow of one training iteration in model parallelism is depicted in *Figure 6.5*. Here, **F1** means Layer 1's forward propagation, which is defined in *Figure 6.3*. Similarly, B1 means Layer 1's backward propagation, which is defined in *Figure 6.4*.

The whole workflow of one training iteration shown in *Figure 6.5* is as follows:

- During the forward propagation, the execution order is **F1->F2->F3**.
- During the backward propagation, the execution order is **B3->B2->B1**.

As you can see from the preceding execution order, the execution order of backward propagation is the inverse of forward propagation. The differing execution order of forward and backward propagation in model parallelism training is one of the causes of system inefficiency.

There is plenty of GPU idle time among all three GPUs in use. For example, **GPU1** is idle between the processing of **F1** and **B1** in *Figure 6.5*.

In *Figure 6.6*, we highlight all the time periods that each GPU is idle in, which are denoted by the double-arrow lines.

Let's look at each GPU's idle time in *Figure 6.6*:

- **GPU 1**: Idle between **F1** and **B1**
- **GPU 2**: Idle during the **F1** period, also between the **F2** and **B2** period, and the **B1** period
- **GPU 3**: Idle during the **F1**, **F2**, **B2**, and **B1** periods

To check how much time is spent idling, let's assume that each GPU's forward and backward propagation times are the same.

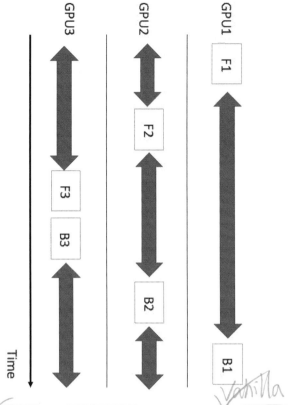

Figure 6.6 – GPU idle time in one training iteration with model parallelism

As shown in *Figure 6.6*, we can calculate each GPU's working and idle times as follows:

- **GPU1**: Working in the **F1** and **B1** time slots, idle in the **F2, F3, B3, B2** time slots
- **GPU2:** Working in the **F2** and **B2** time slots, idle in the **F1, F3, B3, B1** time slots
- **GPU3**: Working in the **F3** and **B3** time slots, idle in the **F1, F2, B2, B1** time slots

As per the GPU working/idle times in the preceding list, given the assumption that the forward propagation time is equal to the backward propagation time, we can conclude that every GPU works for 1/3 of the time of one training iteration, and is idle for 2/3 of the time in one training iteration. Therefore, with vanilla model parallelism training, the average GPU utilization is only around 33%, which is very low.

The main reason for this inefficiency is that GPUs with different model partitions need to wait for each other. To be more specific, in our *Figure 6.6* example, we have the following:

- After the execution of **F1**, **GPU 1** needs to wait for **B2** to complete.

- **GPU 2's F2** needs to wait for **GPU1's F1** to complete, and **GPU2's B2** needs to wait for GPU 3's B3 to complete.

- **GPU3's F3** needs to wait for **GPU2's F2** to complete.

This sequential layer dependency is the main reason for system inefficiency.

> **Vanilla Model Parallelism Training Is Inefficient**
>
> The main reason is the sequential layer dependency. Layer dependency means that GPUs with different model partitions need to wait for other GPUs' intermediate outputs.

Note that in the preceding cases we only used three GPUs. This system inefficiency can be more severe when more GPUs are involved in a model parallelism training job.

For example, let's assume we have a 10-layer **deep neural network** (**DNN**) model, and we split each layer into a single GPU. Let's still assume each layer's forward propagation and backward propagation take roughly the same amount of time. Then, for one training iteration, the total amount of time is 20 time slots: 10 for 10 layers' forward propagation, and another 10 time slots for 10 layers' backward propagation. However, each GPU only works for 2 time slots and is idle for the other 18 time slots. The two working time slots are one for its local forward propagation and the other for its local backward propagation. Therefore, each GPU's utilization rate is only 10%.

With the assumption that each GPU's forward and backward propagation take the same amount of time with N GPUs in use, we can get the following equation:

$$total\_time \; = \; 2 * N$$

The preceding equation is similar to the 10-GPU example mentioned previously. Basically, with N GPUs in use, we need N time slots to finish the whole forward propagation of the model, and another N time slots to finish the backward propagation of the whole model. Each GPU's working time is depicted in the following equation;

$$GPU\_work \; = \; 2$$

Basically, each GPU only works for two time slots: one for forward propagation, and the other for backward propagation. Now, we calculate each GPU's idle time using the following equation:

$$GPU\_idle = 2 * (N - 1)$$

For each GPU, during the entire N time slots' forward propagation, it only works for 1 time slot, and remains idle for the rest of the *N-1* time slots. Similarly, for the backward propagation, each GPU only works for 1 time slot, and remains idle for the remaining *N-1* time slots. Therefore, in total, each GPU's idle time is *(N-1) + (N-1) = 2 * (N-1)*.

Now we can calculate each GPU's utilization rate with the following equation:

$$GPU\_util = \frac{GPU\_work}{total\_time} = \frac{2}{2 * N} = \frac{1}{N}$$

Given the preceding equation, the more GPUs we use for the same model parallelism training, the lower the GPU utilization rate each GPU will have. For example, say we use 100 GPUs to train a giant NLP model and we use model parallelism training to split the model layer-wise among 100 GPUs. In this case, for each GPU, the utilization rate is only 1%. It is definitely not acceptable because each GPU idles for 99% of the total training time.

> **GPU Utilization Rate in Vanilla Model Parallel Training**
>
> To simplify the problem, we assume that each GPU's forward propagation and backward propagation times are the same. Given N GPUs in use for the same model parallelism training job, we can conclude that each GPU's utilization rate is 1/N.

As you can now see the inefficiency problem in vanilla model parallelism training, next, we will discuss several widely adopted approaches to improve system efficiency in model parallelism training.

The first one we will introduce is called **pipeline parallelism**. Pipeline parallelism tries to pipeline the input processing during both the forward and backward propagation of model parallelism training.

After that, we will talk about recent techniques for improving model parallelism training by splitting the layers of each NLP model.

Pipeline input

In this section, we will explain how **pipeline parallelism** works. At a high level, pipeline parallelism breaks each batch of training input into smaller micro-batches and conducts data pipelining over these micro-batches. To illustrate it more clearly, let's first describe how normal batch training works.

We will use the three-layer model example depicted in *Figure 6.1*. We will also maintain the GPU setup depicted in *Figure 6.2*.

Now assume that each training batch contains three input items: input 1, input 2, and input 3. We use this batch to feed in the model. We draw the forward propagation workflow as shown in *Figure 6.7*. It works as follows:

1. After **GPU1** receives the training batch of inputs 1, 2, and 3, **GPU1** conducts forward propagation as **F1i** (forward propagation on input **i** on **GPU1**), which is, **F11**, **F12**, and **F13**.

2. After **GPU1** finishes the forward propagation of inputs 1, 2, and 3, it passes its layer output of **F11**, **F12**, **F13** to **GPU2**. Based on **GPU1**'s output, **GPU2** starts the forward propagation of **F2i** (forward propagation based on input **i**'s data on **GPU2**) as **F21**, **F22**, and **F23**.

3. After **GPU2** finishes its forward propagation, **GPU3** works on its local forward propagation as **F3i** (forward propagation based on input **i** on **GPU3**) as **F31**, **F32**, and **F33**.

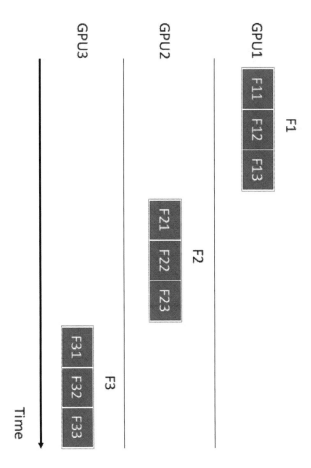

Figure 6.7 – Forward propagation of model parallelism training with an input batch size of 3

As shown in *Figure 6.7*, each input is being processed sequentially. This sequential data processing remains in the backward propagation, as shown in the following diagram:

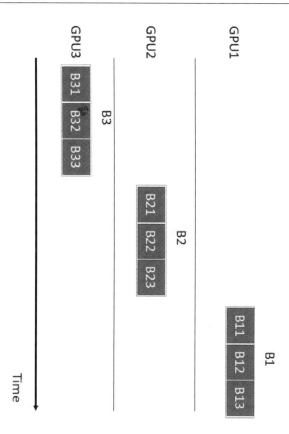

Figure 6.8 – Backward propagation of model parallelism training with an input batch size of 3

As shown in the preceding diagram, during the backward propagation, **GPU3** first calculates the gradients based on inputs 1, 2, and 3 sequentially. Then, **GPU2** starts calculating its local gradients based on inputs 1, 2, and 3. Finally, **GPU1** starts calculating the gradients based on inputs 1, 2, and 3.

In *Figures 6.7 and 6.8*, we just zoomed in to take a look at what is inside each **Fi** and **Bi** in *Figures 6.4, 6.5,* and *6.6* (where i is inputs 1, 2, 3). Now we will discuss how we can do data pipelining with these three input data items.

Let's first look at how to do data pipelining in the forward propagation of *Figure 6.7*. As shown in *Figure 6.9*, the data pipeline of forward propagation works on input 1 and is illustrated as follows:

1. **GPU1** first calculates **F11** based on input 1. After this is done, **GPU1** will pass its layer output of **F11** to **GPU2**.

2. After receiving **GPU1**'s **F11** output, **GPU2** can start working on **F21**, which can happen when **GPU1** is working on **F12**.

3. After **GPU2** is done processing **F21**, **GPU2** can pass its layer output of **F21** to **GPU3**.

4. After **GPU3** receives **GPU2**'s **F21** output, **GPU3** can start working on **F31**, which can happen simultaneously with **GPU2**'s processing of **F22**.

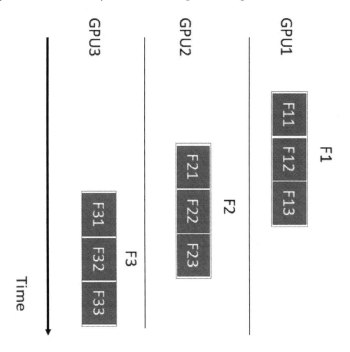

Figure 6.9 – Pipeline parallelism for forward propagation

Comparing the forward propagation in *Figure 6.9* with data pipelining and *Figure 6.7* without pipelining, we can clearly see the end-to-end time difference. For the sake of illustration, we also assume that processing each input data item takes the same amount of time.

As shown in *Figure 6.7*, without pipeline parallelism, it takes 9 time slots to finish the whole forward propagation with a batch size of 3. However, as shown in *Figure 6.9*, by adopting pipeline parallelism, it only takes 5 time slots to finish the whole forward propagation with the same batch size of 3.

Therefore, adopting pipeline parallelism significantly reduces the total training time (for example, from 9 time slots to 5 in our example). Similar things happen during backward propagation. We illustrate pipeline parallelism of backward propagation as follows:

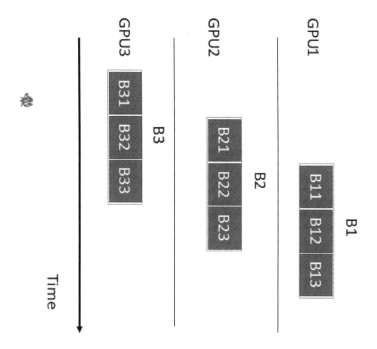

Figure 6.10 – Pipeline parallelism for backward propagation

By comparing *Figure 6.8* and *Figure 6.10*, we can see that adopting pipeline parallelism during backward propagation reduces the total training time as well. In our batch size 3 example, with pipeline parallelism, we can reduce the overall backward propagation from 9 time slots (*Figure 6.8*) to just 5 time slots (*Figure 6.10*).

Next, we will discuss the pros and cons of pipeline parallelism.

Pros and cons of pipeline parallelism

In the preceding sections, we discussed how pipeline parallelism works in both forward and backward propagation during model parallelism training. In this section, we will discuss the advantages and disadvantages of pipeline parallelism.

Advantages of pipeline parallelism

The most important advantage of pipeline parallelism is that it helps to reduce the GPU idle time during model parallelism training. Here, we list all the advantages:

- Reduces overall training time
- Reduces GPU idle time while waiting for the predecessor or successor's GPU output

- Not much coding complexity to implement pipeline parallelism

- Can be generally adapted to any kind of DNN model

- Simple and easy to understand

Disadvantages of pipeline parallelism

In the preceding section, we discussed the advantages of pipeline parallelism. Now let's look at the disadvantages of pipeline parallelism:

- The CPU needs to send more instructions to GPUs. For example, if we break 1 input batch into N micro-batches for pipeline parallelism, the CPU needs to send N-1 times more instructions to each GPU.

- Although pipeline parallelism reduces the GPU idle time, there is still GPU idle time. For example, in *Figure 6.9*, **GPU3** still needs to wait for **F11** and **F21** to finish. Also, during the **F11** and **F21** time slots, **GPU3** remains idle.

- Pipeline parallelism introduces more frequent GPU communications. For example, in *Figure 6.9*, during forward propagation, **GPU1** needed to send its outputs to **GPU2** three times (once for each input). However, in vanilla model parallelism training, as shown in *Figure 6.7*, **GPU1** just needed to send its outputs to **GPU2** once (which includes all three inputs). More frequent small data transmission introduces a high networking communication overhead. This is mainly because small data chunks may not fully saturate the link bandwidth.

Next, we will discuss another methodology to improve system efficiency in model parallelism training, which is called intra-layer parallelism.

Layer split *tensor parallelism*

In this section, we will discuss another kind of approach to improve model parallelism training efficiency called **intra-layer model parallelism**. Generally speaking, the data structure for holding each layer's neurons can be represented as **matrices**. One common function during NLP model training and serving is **matrix multiplication**. Therefore, we can split a layer's matrix in some way to enable in-parallel execution.

Let's discuss it with a simple example. Let's just focus on **Layer 1** of any model. It takes the training data as input, and after forward propagation, it generates some outputs to the following layers. We can draw this **Layer 1** as shown in *Figure 6.11*:

Layer 1 Matrix

w(0,0)	w(1,0)	w(2,0)	w(3,0)
w(0,1)	w(1,1)	w(2,1)	w(3,1)
w(0,2)	w(1,2)	w(2,2)	w(3,2)
w(0,3)	w(1,3)	w(2,3)	w(3,3)

Figure 6.11 – Weights matrix for Layer 1 of an NLP model

As shown in *Figure 6.11*, we illustrate the data structure that represents **Layer 1** of an NLP model. Here, each column represents a neuron. Each weight within a column is a neuron weight. Basically, in this setting, we have four neurons and each neuron has four weights inside.

Now, let's assume we have input with a batch size of 4, as shown in *Figure 6.12*:

Input Matrix (batch size = 4)

x(0,0)	x(0,1)	w(0,2)	w(0,3)
x(1,0)	x(1,1)	x(1,2)	x(1,3)
x(2,0)	x(2,1)	x(2,2)	x(2,3)
x(3,0)	x(3,1)	x(3,2)	x(3,3)

Figure 6.12 – Input data matrix with a batch size of 4

As shown in the preceding figure, we have an input data matrix of 4 x 4. Here, each row is a single input data item. For NLP, you can regard each row as an embedded sentence. Here, we have four input data items within this batch. Each data item has four values, which can be regarded as four word embeddings within a sentence.

Here, the forward propagation can be regarded as a matrix multiplication between Layer 1's weight and input batch, which is defined as follows:

$$y = X * A$$

Here, y means **Layer 1**'s output to the next layer.

What intra-layer split really does is the following:

1. We split the **Layer 1** matrix along its columns. For example, we split **Layer 1**'s columns into two halves. Then, A can be written as A_01, A_23, as in in *Figure 6.13*. Basically, each split layer maintains only two neurons of the original **Layer 1.**

2. By splitting **Layer 1** column-wise into two halves, we pass input X and calculate y as follows:

$$y\_01, y\_23 = [X * A\_01, X * A\_23]$$

3. Then, **Layer 1** passes *[y_01, y_23]* as the output to **Layer 2.**

By splitting the model layer in this way, we can partition the model not only for each layer but also within each layer. The intra-layer split of **Layer 1** can be done as shown in the following figure:

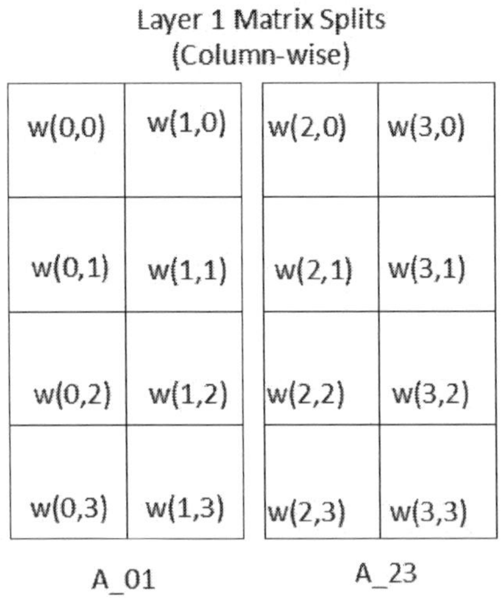

Layer 1 Matrix Splits
(Column-wise)

w(0,0)	w(1,0)	w(2,0)	w(3,0)
w(0,1)	w(1,1)	w(2,1)	w(3,1)
w(0,2)	w(1,2)	w(2,2)	w(3,2)
w(0,3)	w(1,3)	w(2,3)	w(3,3)

A_01   A_23

Figure 6.13 – Intra-layer split for layer 1 (column-wise split)

The following layers can do the same thing as **Layer 1.** You can simply regard the *X* matrix as the previous layer's output. In addition, if the previous layer is split by layer to match the shape dimension of the matrix multiplication, you will need to split the current layer along the row dimension.

By doing this intra-layer split of the model, we can achieve model parallelism acting without communication among the model partitions on each GPU. This is really important since communications are always expensive, especially in latency-driven application scenarios.

Notes on intra-layer model parallelism

Here, we will discuss some more details of intra-layer model parallelism.

Intra-layer model parallelism is a good way to split giant NLP models. This is because it allows model partitioning within a layer and without introducing significant communication overhead during forward and backward propagation. Basically, for one split, it may only introduce one All-Reduce function in either forward or backward propagation, which is acceptable.

In addition, intra-layer model parallelism can also be easily adopted together with data parallelism training. If we have a multi-machine, multi-GPU system, we can do intra-layer parallelism within a machine. This is because GPUs within a machine often have high communication bandwidth. We can also do data parallelism training across different machines.

Finally, we generally believe intra-layer model parallelism is mostly applicable to NLP models. In other words, for **convolutional neural network** (**CNN**) or **reinforcement learning** (**RL**) models, there may be cases where intra-layer parallelism does not work.

Summary

In this chapter, we discussed ways to improve system efficiency in model parallelism training.

After reading through this chapter, you should understand why vanilla model parallelism is very inefficient. You should also have learned two techniques to improve system efficiency in model parallelism training. One is pipeline parallelism; the other is intra-layer split methods.

In the next chapter, we will discuss how to implement a model parallelism training and serving pipeline.

7
Implementing Model Parallel Training and Serving Workflows

In this chapter, we will discuss how to implement a simple model parallelism pipeline. As opposed to data parallelism, where each GPU holds a full copy of a model, in model parallelism, we need to split a model properly among all GPUs in use.

Before diving into the details, we'll qualify our discussion with the following assumptions about both hardware and workload:

- We will use homogenous GPUs for the same model parallel training or serving job.

- Each model training or serving task will occupy the whole hardware exclusively, which means there will be no preemption or interruption during the running of our model training or serving task.

- For GPUs within a machine, they are connected with either PCIe, NVLink, or NVSwitch.

- For GPUs among different machines, they are connected with general Ethernet links of 10 Gbps to 100 Gbps bandwidth.

- For the model parallel training part, we will mainly focus on the fine-tuning stage rather than the pre-training stage.

- For each training batch, we will properly set a good batch size so that it will not cause an out-of-memory error.

- Each model may have different variations (for example, BERT has BERT base and BERT large). We will choose the proper version of the model so that it will not cause an out-of-memory issue during both the model fine-tuning and serving stages.

This chapter focuses on implementation of model parallel training and serving. First, we will illustrate the whole pipeline for model training and serving, which includes model split and deploy, and training and serving workflows. Second, we will fine-tune a language model. Third, we will discuss hyperparameters regarding model parallel training. Fourth, we will launch some model parallel serving tasks for model testing and evaluations.

In a nutshell, you will learn the following topics in this chapter:

- Wrapping up the whole model parallelism pipeline

- Fine-tuning transformers

- Hyperparameter tuning in model parallelism

- NLP model serving

First, we will first wrap up the whole workflow of model parallel training and serving. Then, we will discuss how to do transformer fine-tuning, hyperparameter tuning, and NLP model serving.

Technical requirements

For implementation in the rest of the sections, we may illustrate this using the BERT or GPT models. We will use the **Stanford Question Answering Dataset (SquAD)** 2.0 as our dataset and PyTorch for illustration. The main library dependencies for our code are as follows:

- `torch>=1.7.1`

- `transformers>=4.10.3`

- `cuda>=11.0`

- `torchvision>=0.9.1`

- `Nvidia driver >=450.119.03`

It is mandatory to have the correct versions of the preceding libraries installed before moving ahead with this chapter.

Wrapping up the whole model parallelism pipeline

In this section, we will discuss the components for implementing model parallelism. We will first discuss how to implement a model parallel training pipeline and then how to implement a model parallel serving pipeline.

A model parallel training overview

Let's look at a simple example of model parallel training, as shown in the following diagram:

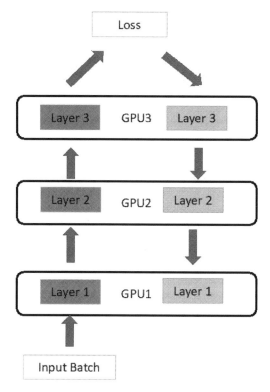

Figure 7.1 – Model parallel training on a three-layer deep neural network (DNN) model

As shown in the preceding diagram, we have a three-layer DNN model, and we split each layer onto one GPU. For example, we put **Layer 1** on **GPU1** and **Layer 2** on **GPU2**.

Forward propagation in model parallel training is shown on the left side of *Figure 7.1*. It works as follows:

1. After **GPU1** consumes the input training batch, it will calculate the activation values of **Layer 1**.

2. After **GPU2** receives output from **GPU1**, **GPU2** starts its own forward propagation, which generates the local activation and output of **Layer 2** to **Layer 3**.

3. After **GPU3** receives output from **GPU2**, **GPU3** starts its own forward propagation and generates prediction output.

Backward propagation is shown on the right-hand side of *Figure 7.1*. It works as follows:

1. After **GPU3** generates the local gradients of **Layer 3**, it passes the gradient outputs to **GPU2**.

2. After **GPU2** receives outputs from **GPU3**, **GPU2** calculates its local gradients for **Layer 2** and generates gradient output to **GPU1**.

3. After **GPU1** receives outputs from **GPU2**, **GPU 1** calculates its local gradients for **Layer 1**.

4. Then, we can use each layer's local gradients to update the corresponding model parameters.

The preceding steps define the whole model parallel training workflow, as shown in *Figure 7.1*.

Implementing a model parallel training pipeline

Now, let's look at how to implement such a model parallel training pipeline.

For ease of understanding, we will use a simple DNN model. The model structure is defined in the following diagram:

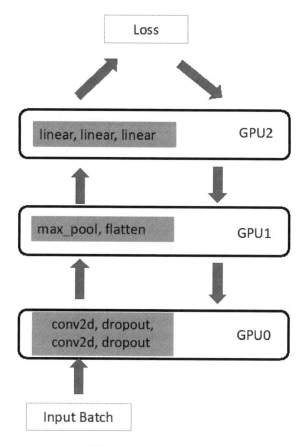

Figure 7.2 – Model parallel training for a real DNN model

As shown in the preceding diagram, we split a DNN model into three GPUs, which look similar to *Figure 7.1*. As shown in *Figure 7.2*, each GPU actually holds multiple sequential layers rather than just one layer (as seen in *Figure 7.1*).

More specifically, the DNN layer layout in *Figure 7.2* is listed as follows:

- **GPU0** holds two conv2d layers and two dropout layers.
- **GPU1** holds one maxpool layer and one flatten layer.
- **GPU2** holds three fully connected (linear) layers.

To implement the model defined in *Figure 7.2*, we use the corresponding PyTorch code:

```python
import torch
import torch.nn as nn
import torch.nn.functional as F

class MyNet(nn.Module):
    def __init__(self):
        super(MyNet, self).__init__()
        self.seq1 = nn.Sequential(
                        nn.Conv2d(1,32,3,1),
                        nn.Dropout2d(0.5),
                        nn.Conv2d(32,64,3,1),
                        nn.Dropout2d(0.75)).to('cuda:0')
        self.seq2 = nn.Sequential(
                        nn.Linear(9216, 128),
                        nn.Linear(128,20),
                        nn.Linear(20,10)).to('cuda:2')

    def forward(self, x):
        x = self.seq1(x.to('cuda:0'))
        x = F.max_pool2d(x,2).to('cuda:1')
        x = torch.flatten(x,1).to('cuda:1')
        x = self.seq2(x.to('cuda:2'))
        output = F.log_softmax(x, dim = 1)
        return output
```

Figure 7.3 – PyTorch implementation for model splits

As shown in the preceding screenshot, we implement our model split as follows:

- We define seq1() as the layers we put on GPU0.

- We define seq2() as the linear layers we put on GPU2.

- In the forward() function, we define F.max_pool2d() and torch.flatten() as the layers we put on GPU1.

In the `forward()` function, we also define the sequential order of the layers holding on different GPUs, as follows:

1. We pass the input data into GPU0 as the `x.to('cuda:0')` function.

2. After the `seq1()` function, we pass the GPU0's output to GPU1, as follows:

```
x = F.max_pool2d(x,2).to('cuda:1')
x = torch.flatten(x,1).to('cuda:1')
```

3. Then, we pass GPU1's output to GPU2 as the `x.to('cuda:2')` function.

So far, we have defined the forward propagation layer sequence and GPU allocations. Then, PyTorch or TensorFlow can automatically generate the corresponding backward propagation layer order. Thus, we do not need to specify the inverse order of layer dependency during the backward propagation.

Specifying communication protocol among GPUs

Next, we also need to change the model train function so that it will know which GPU we should pass in the training input and from which GPU we can get the prediction results.

The code for specifying which GPU takes input data and which GPU generates the final prediction results is as follows:

```
# Model Parallel Training
def train(args):
...
    criterion = nn.CrossEntropyLoss()
    optimizer = torch.optim.SGD(model.parameters(), lr = 1e-3)
...

    for epoch in range(args.epochs):
        print(f"Epoch {epoch}")
        for idx, (data, target) in enumerate(trainloader):
            data = data.to('cuda:0')
            optimizer.zero_grad()
            output = model(data)
            target = target.to(output.device)
            loss = F.cross_entropy(output, target)
            loss.backward()
```

```
        optimizer.step()
        print(f"batch {idx} training :: loss {loss.
item()}")
    print("Training Done!")
  return model
```

As shown in the preceding code segment, we implement our model parallel training function with the following steps:

1. We first define the loss function as `criterion = nn.CrossEntropyLoss()`.

2. Then, we need to define our training optimizer as `optimizer = torch.optim.SGD(model.parameters(), lr = 1e-3)`.

3. Within our training loop, we move the data to GPU0 as `data = data.to('cuda:0')`.

4. Finally, we need to define the GPU that generates a prediction as `target = target.to(output.device)`. Here, `output.device` automatically tracks that the GPU2 is the output device and passes the target to GPU2.

With the preceding code pieces inside the `train()` function, we can now run the model parallel training job using three GPUs (GPU0, GPU1, and GPU2).

The running screenshots are shown as follows:

```
Epoch 0
batch 0 training :: loss 2.367696523666382
batch 1 training :: loss 2.358067274093628
batch 2 training :: loss 2.3166911602020264
batch 3 training :: loss 2.3472657203674316
batch 4 training :: loss 2.3291213512420654
batch 5 training :: loss 2.341862201690674
batch 6 training :: loss 2.3476767539978027
batch 7 training :: loss 2.3589253425598145
batch 8 training :: loss 2.3385939598083496
batch 9 training :: loss 2.314199209213257
batch 10 training :: loss 2.357100486755371
batch 11 training :: loss 2.341332197189331
batch 12 training :: loss 2.3510727882385254
batch 13 training :: loss 2.305490732192993
batch 14 training :: loss 2.2896692752838135
batch 15 training :: loss 2.2965853214263916
batch 16 training :: loss 2.289027452468872
batch 17 training :: loss 2.318589687347412
batch 18 training :: loss 2.314786911010742
batch 19 training :: loss 2.292377471923828
batch 20 training :: loss 2.311783790588379
batch 21 training :: loss 2.3006303310394287
batch 22 training :: loss 2.2897908687591553
batch 23 training :: loss 2.309767246246338
batch 24 training :: loss 2.326434373855591
batch 25 training :: loss 2.3054540157318115
batch 26 training :: loss 2.3287947177886963
batch 27 training :: loss 2.309558391571045
batch 28 training :: loss 2.289318084716797
batch 29 training :: loss 2.3383259773254395
batch 30 training :: loss 2.2959561347961426
batch 31 training :: loss 2.2574143409729004
batch 32 training :: loss 2.293168783187866
batch 33 training :: loss 2.2815194129943848
batch 34 training :: loss 2.2899670600891113
batch 35 training :: loss 2.2440366744995117
batch 36 training :: loss 2.2733407020568848
batch 37 training :: loss 2.2578611373901367
batch 38 training :: loss 2.2523033618927
batch 39 training :: loss 2.2961771488189697
batch 40 training :: loss 2.269951820373535
```

Figure 7.4 – The first 40 training batches

The preceding screenshot shows that we started the model parallel training successfully. After training several iterations, we can see the loss value decrease to less than 0.5, which is shown in the following screenshot:

```
batch 450 training :: loss 0.4500477612018585
batch 451 training :: loss 0.41694992780685425
batch 452 training :: loss 0.5335432291030884
batch 453 training :: loss 0.3785797357559204
batch 454 training :: loss 0.5250097513198853
batch 455 training :: loss 0.48590853810310364
batch 456 training :: loss 0.4359087646007538
batch 457 training :: loss 0.5516181588172913
batch 458 training :: loss 0.4193853735923767
batch 459 training :: loss 0.24893827736377716
batch 460 training :: loss 0.4412848949432373
batch 461 training :: loss 0.6855418086051941
batch 462 training :: loss 0.60863196849823
batch 463 training :: loss 0.6327939629554749
batch 464 training :: loss 0.4109138548374176
batch 465 training :: loss 0.3921489715576172
batch 466 training :: loss 0.3610058128833771
batch 467 training :: loss 0.4983370304107666
batch 468 training :: loss 0.497358113527298
Training Done!
```

Figure 7.5 – The last 18 training batches

The preceding screenshot verifies that our implementation of model parallel training is correct, and the model can be converged after training.

Additionally, to verify whether this training job really uses three GPUs simultaneously, we can open another terminal to monitor the GPU utilization using the watch nvidia-smi function. The following is a screenshot of the monitoring of nvidia-smi:

```
+-----------------------------------------------------------------------------+
| NVIDIA-SMI 450.142.00    Driver Version: 450.142.00    CUDA Version: 11.0    |
|-------------------------------+----------------------+----------------------+
| GPU  Name        Persistence-M| Bus-Id        Disp.A | Volatile Uncorr. ECC |
| Fan  Temp  Perf  Pwr:Usage/Cap|         Memory-Usage | GPU-Util  Compute M. |
|                               |                      |               MIG M. |
|===============================+======================+======================|
|   0  Tesla M60           On   | 00000000:00:1B.0 Off |                    0 |
| N/A   32C    P0    82W / 150W |   1008MiB /  7618MiB |      69%     Default |
|                               |                      |                  N/A |
+-------------------------------+----------------------+----------------------+
|   1  Tesla M60           On   | 00000000:00:1C.0 Off |                    0 |
| N/A   25C    P0    38W / 150W |    708MiB /  7618MiB |      18%     Default |
|                               |                      |                  N/A |
+-------------------------------+----------------------+----------------------+
|   2  Tesla M60           On   | 00000000:00:1D.0 Off |                    0 |
| N/A   29C    P0    39W / 150W |    772MiB /  7618MiB |      21%     Default |
|                               |                      |                  N/A |
+-------------------------------+----------------------+----------------------+
|   3  Tesla M60           On   | 00000000:00:1E.0 Off |                    0 |
| N/A   23C    P8    14W / 150W |      3MiB /  7618MiB |       0%     Default |
|                               |                      |                  N/A |
+-------------------------------+----------------------+----------------------+

+-----------------------------------------------------------------------------+
| Processes:                                                                  |
|  GPU   GI   CI        PID   Type   Process name                  GPU Memory |
|        ID   ID                                                   Usage      |
|=============================================================================|
|    0   N/A  N/A       722     C   python                            1005MiB |
|    1   N/A  N/A       722     C   python                             705MiB |
|    2   N/A  N/A       722     C   python                             769MiB |
+-----------------------------------------------------------------------------+
```

Figure 7.6 – Concurrent model training using three GPUs

As shown in the preceding screenshot, we use three GPUs (**0**, **1**, and **2**) together to run the same model parallel training job.

Next, we will discuss how to implement model parallel serving. By splitting a model into multiple GPUs, we coordinate all the GPUs in order to finish the model parallel serving job.

Model parallel serving

In the previous section, we discussed how to use three GPUs together to conduct a model parallel training job. Now, we will assume that the model is fully trained. We will split this fully trained model into multiple GPUs for model parallel serving. In contrast with the model parallel training shown in *Figure 7.1*, here, we draw the model parallel serving diagram:

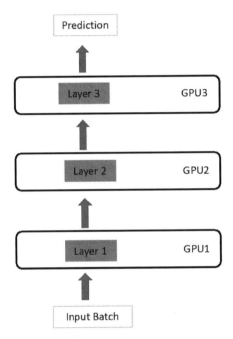

Figure 7.7 – Model parallel serving in a three-GPU setting

As shown in the preceding diagram, in contrast to the model parallel training shown in *Figure 7.1*, there is no backward propagation in model parallel serving. As depicted in *Figure 7.7*, given the input data batch, we pass it over different layers held by different GPUs and only conduct forward propagation. After the forward propagation finishes, the last layer on GPU3 will generate our prediction results.

To implement model parallel serving, we still use the model we have used for model parallel training. The model structure is defined in *Figure 7.2* and *Figure 7.7*. On the code side, we do not need to change anything in the model structure. The only thing we need to change is the model serving function:

1.   The code snippet for implementing model parallel serving is as follows:

```
# Model Parallel Serving
def test(args, model):
```

```
...
    model.eval()
...
    correct_total = 0
...
    with torch.no_grad():
        for idx, (data, target) in enumerate(testloader):
            output = model(data.to('cuda:0'))
            predict = output.argmax(dim=1,
                    keepdim=True).to(output.device)
            target = target.to(output.device)
            correct = predict.eq(target.view_as(predict))
                    .sum().item()
            correct_total += correct
        acc = correct_total/len(testloader.dataset)
        print(f"Test Accuracy {acc}")
    print("Test Done!")
...
```

2. As shown in the preceding code snippet, we first need to set the model to the serving stage, as follows:

```
model.eval()
```

3. Then, we will use the test loader to load test data into the fully trained model. Note that since we split the model layer-wise, we need to make sure that the test data is passing into GPU0 and not any other GPUs. We enforce it by doing the following:

```
output = model(data.to('cuda:0'))
```

Basically, we enforce the input data to be passed to GPU0 (that is, `cuda:0`).

4. After that, we need to specify from which GPU we can get the model prediction results. It is specified as follows:

```
predict = output.argmax(dim=1, keepdim=True)
        .to(output.device)
```

Here, `output.device` guarantees that we can collect our prediction results on GPU2 since it is the final output device (that is, the device that holds the last layer of the model).

5.   Next, we need to pass the true label to the output device so that we can calculate the accuracy by doing the following:

$$accuracy = \frac{\# \ of \ (prediction == label)}{total \ data \ size}$$

Basically, the accuracy will count how many times our model prediction equals the true label. Then, we use this count value divided by the total test data size to calculate accuracy.

6.   Thus, we also need to make sure that the true label is passed into our GPU2. We enforce it with the following code:

```
target = target.to(output.device)
```

After finishing all the things here, we now can conduct model parallel serving using our previously trained model.

When you start running model serving, you will see the following printout in the terminal:

```
Test Accuracy 0.0019666666666666665
Test Accuracy 0.0037333333333333333
Test Accuracy 0.005683333333333334
Test Accuracy 0.0076
Test Accuracy 0.009483333333333333
Test Accuracy 0.0114
Test Accuracy 0.013216666666666666
Test Accuracy 0.015066666666666667
Test Accuracy 0.0168
Test Accuracy 0.01875
Test Accuracy 0.020566666666666667
Test Accuracy 0.0225
Test Accuracy 0.0243
Test Accuracy 0.026333333333333334
```

Figure 7.8 – Test accuracy starts increasing

As you can see, the test accuracy starts increasing because we have more and more correct prediction results.

Once the whole test finishes, you will see that the test accuracy reaches a reasonably good number, as shown in the following screenshot:

```
Test Accuracy 0.8768166666666667
Test Accuracy 0.8786333333333334
Test Accuracy 0.88055
Test Accuracy 0.8826333333333334
Test Accuracy 0.8844666666666666
Test Accuracy 0.8865666666666666
Test Accuracy 0.88795
Test Done!
```

Figure 7.9 – The model test finishes

As shown in the preceding screenshot, we achieve 88.79% model serving accuracy with our model parallel serving pipeline.

To verify whether we have used all the three GPUs together, we can do the same system resource monitoring using nvidia-smi. The result is shown as follows:

```
+-----------------------------------------------------------------------------+
| NVIDIA-SMI 450.142.00   Driver Version: 450.142.00   CUDA Version: 11.0     |
|-------------------------------+----------------------+----------------------+
| GPU  Name        Persistence-M| Bus-Id        Disp.A | Volatile Uncorr. ECC |
| Fan  Temp  Perf  Pwr:Usage/Cap|         Memory-Usage | GPU-Util  Compute M. |
|                               |                      |               MIG M. |
|===============================+======================+======================|
|   0  Tesla M60            On  | 00000000:00:1B.0 Off |                    0 |
| N/A   38C    P0    78W / 150W |   1008MiB /  7618MiB |     42%      Default |
|                               |                      |                  N/A |
+-------------------------------+----------------------+----------------------+
|   1  Tesla M60            On  | 00000000:00:1C.0 Off |                    0 |
| N/A   27C    P0    38W / 150W |    708MiB /  7618MiB |     20%      Default |
|                               |                      |                  N/A |
+-------------------------------+----------------------+----------------------+
|   2  Tesla M60            On  | 00000000:00:1D.0 Off |                    0 |
| N/A   30C    P0    39W / 150W |    772MiB /  7618MiB |     21%      Default |
|                               |                      |                  N/A |
+-------------------------------+----------------------+----------------------+
|   3  Tesla M60            On  | 00000000:00:1E.0 Off |                    0 |
| N/A   23C    P8    14W / 150W |      3MiB /  7618MiB |      0%      Default |
|                               |                      |                  N/A |
+-------------------------------+----------------------+----------------------+

+-----------------------------------------------------------------------------+
| Processes:                                                                  |
|  GPU   GI   CI        PID   Type   Process name                  GPU Memory |
|        ID   ID                                                   Usage      |
|=============================================================================|
|    0   N/A  N/A     10485      C   python                           1005MiB |
|    1   N/A  N/A     10485      C   python                            705MiB |
|    2   N/A  N/A     10485      C   python                            769MiB |
+-----------------------------------------------------------------------------+
```

Figure 7.10 – Model parallel training using GPUs 0, 1, and 2

As shown in the preceding screenshot, we have three GPUs working simultaneously on the same model serving job. This verifies the correctness of our model parallel serving implementation.

In this section, we discussed how to implement a model parallel training pipeline and how to implement a model parallel serving pipeline.

Next, we will discuss how to do fine-tuning on transformers.

Fine-tuning transformers

In this section, we will discuss how to conduct fine-tuning on pre-trained transformer models. Here, we mainly focus on the BERT model, which is fully trained, and we will work on the SQuAD 2.0 dataset.

The whole code base for running custom training on the BERT model can be easily found on the Hugging Face website (`https://huggingface.co/transformers/custom_datasets.html#qa-squad`). Our previous model parallelism implementation can be directly applied to this code base to speed up model training and serving.

Here, we highlight the important steps in the workflow of fine-tuning BERT on SQuAD 2.0. The overview is shown in the following screenshot:

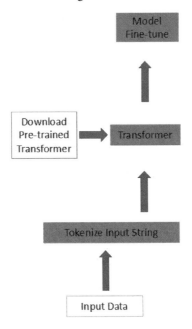

Figure 7.11 – Fine-tuning the transformer on downstream tasks

As shown in the preceding screenshot, the whole fine-tuning process involves three steps, as follows:

1. Tokenize the input string.
2. Download the pre-trained base model.
3. Then, use the tokenized input to do fine-tuning on the pre-trained model.

By adopting these three steps, we can finish transformer fine-tuning on a custom dataset such as SQuAD 2.0.

Next, we will discuss the important hyperparameters during model parallel training.

Hyperparameter tuning in model parallelism

In this section, we will discuss some of the important hyperparameters required during the model parallel training process, such as balancing the workload among GPUs and enabling/disabling pipeline parallelism.

Balancing the workload among GPUs

In most of the cases, we split the model layer-wise. Since we use homogenous GPUs, we should try to balance the workload among all the GPUs we have.

GPU workload is not always linearly proportional to the number of layers held inside the GPU. One way to balance the workload among GPUs is to look at its computation core utilization. This computation utility value can be found in `nvidia-smi`. For example, the following screenshot shows that GPU0 has a greater workload than GPU1 – `Volatile GPU-Util` on GPU0 is `42%`, whereas on GPU1, it is `20%`:

GPU	Name		Persistence-M	Bus-Id	Disp.A	Volatile Uncorr. ECC
Fan	Temp	Perf	Pwr:Usage/Cap		Memory-Usage	GPU-Util Compute M.
						MIG M.
=====	======	======	===============	===================	===============	=====================
0	Tesla M60		On	00000000:00:1B.0 Off		0
N/A	38C	P0	78W / 150W		1008MiB / 7618MiB	42% Default
						N/A
1	Tesla M60		On	00000000:00:1C.0 Off		0
N/A	27C	P0	38W / 150W		708MiB / 7618MiB	20% Default
						N/A

Figure 7.12 – GPUs are underutilized

Thus, we need to move some of the layers originally assigned on GPU0 to GPU1. The ideal case is that all the GPUs should have roughly the same `GPU-Util` percentage.

Enabling/disabling pipeline parallelism

Another important hyperparameter for model parallel training is pipeline parallelism, which we discussed in *Chapter 6, Pipeline Input and Layer Split*. However, we need to consider whether to use pipeline parallelism.

Experiments and studies can be found at `https://pytorch.org/tutorials/intermediate/model_parallel_tutorial.html` that show that incorporating pipeline parallelism may not always improve system utilization. Thus, we should try to both enable and disable pipeline parallelism, and then we can pick the one that has a higher system utilization rate.

Next, we will discuss NLP model serving.

NLP model serving

Now, we will discuss NLP model serving. We will assume that the model has been successfully trained with your own custom data:

1. First, we define our questions and answers, as follows:

    ```
    string1 = "Packt is a publisher"
    string2 = "Who is Packt ?"

    index_tokens = tokenizer.encode(string1, string2, add_
    special_tokens=True)
    ```

    Basically, we define a question-and-answer pair as `string1` and `string2` and then tokenize both strings.

2. Then, we convert the preceding tokens to torch tensors, as follows:

    ```
    tokens_tensors = torch.tensor([index_tokens])
    ```

3. Then, we can conduct NLP model serving for question answering, as follows:

    ```
    with torch.no_grad():
        out = model(tokens_tensors,
                    token_type_ids = segments_tensors)
    ```

```
ans = tokenizer.decode(index_tokens
                [torch.argmax(out.start_logits):
                torch.argmax(out.end_logits)+1])

print(ans)
```

4. Then, we run the preceding code snippets; given our two input strings, we can get `ans` as the following printout:

```
publisher
```

With the preceding steps, we now finish describing how to do NLP model serving.

Summary

In this chapter, we mainly discussed how to implement a model parallel training and serving pipeline.

After reading this chapter, you should be able to split a DNN model into multiple GPUs and conduct model parallel training and serving. In addition, you should also know how to do hyperparameter tuning for model parallel training jobs. Finally, you can easily test your NLP model by running some model serving tasks.

In the next chapter, we will discuss some advanced techniques to further boost the performance of model parallel training and serving.

8
Achieving Higher Throughput and Lower Latency

Generally speaking, model parallelism is less efficient than data parallelism. The main reasons are twofold, as outlined here.

First, the sequential dependency among **deep neural network** (**DNN**) layers holding onto different **graphics processing units** (**GPUs**) limits the performance. One GPU may not start working until its predecessor finishes generating outputs.

Second, the limited GPU memory makes it impossible to train a large input batch in each training iteration. Due to the large size of the model parameters, we can only train small batches of data per training iteration.

Given the preceding two challenges, we try to improve throughput and latency performance by adopting **state-of-the-art** (**SOTA**) techniques, such as freezing layers, model distillations, and more. Before we dive into the details, we'll first illustrate the assumptions for the materials of this chapter, as follows:

- We assume there are no job preemptions or yields during our whole model training and model serving sessions.

- For model training, we focus on the fine-tuning stage of **natural language processing** (**NLP**) models.

- We assume disk storage is **orders-of-magnitude** (**OOMs**) larger than the on-device memory size.

- We assume the **central processing unit** (**CPU**) memory is usually an OOM bigger than the on-device memory size.

- We assume that different layers of the models may converge to near-optimal points at different training iterations.

- We assume that the GPUs we use can do mixed-precision computation—for example, the GPU can easily convert the tensors with FP32 to FP16 (where **FP** stands for **floating-point**) or even INT8 data format (where **INT** stands for **integer**).

- We assume the use of homogeneous GPUs for each of our training jobs.

- For the communication links, we limit ourselves to using **Peripheral Component Interconnect Express** (**PCIe**), NVLink, or NVSwitch for intra-machine communication, and Ethernet or **InfiniBand** (**IB**) for cross-machine data communication.

- The model we used can be easily pruned with some pre-defined model-pruning policy.

In this chapter, we mainly focus on the SOTA techniques for improving system efficiency in model-parallel training and inference. More specifically, we will cover the following topics in this chapter.

First, we will discuss a novel technique called **layer freezing**. Basically, we may delete the intermediate results of some layers that are fully trained. Thus, we may have more space for holding other layers' intermediate results. Second, GPU local memory size is usually small. We want to explore using much larger storage space, such as CPU memory or disk, to store some intermediate results during model training and inference. Third, we want to shrink down the model size itself to thus allow us to feed in more training input per batch for each training iteration. Finally, we will study how to reduce the bit representation of each scalar in the **deep learning** (**DL**) model parameters.

In a nutshell, you will cover the following topics in this chapter:

- Freezing layers

- Exploring memory and storage resources

- Understanding model decomposition and distillation

- Reducing bits in hardware

Now, we will first look at how the layer-freezing technique works in real model-parallel training. Then, we will explore ways to leverage other storage resources in the system, reduce model size per GPU, and reduce bit representation for the model in succession.

Technical requirements

We assume the use of PyTorch as our by-default implementation platform. The main library dependencies for our code are listed as follows:

- `torch` >= 1.7.1

- `transformers` >= 4.10.3

- `cuda` >= 11.0

- `torchvision` >= 0.9.1

- NVIDIA driver >= 450.119.03

It is mandatory to have the preceding libraries pre-installed with the correct versions.

Freezing layers

The first technique we introduce here is called layer freezing. At a high level, we have the assumption that different layers of a model may converge at different stages of the training process. Thus, we can freeze the layers that converge earlier.

Here, freezing refers to the following two operations:

- We abandon the intermediate results on particular layers during forward propagation.
- We may also avoid generating gradients during backward propagation.

We illustrate this technique in the following diagram:

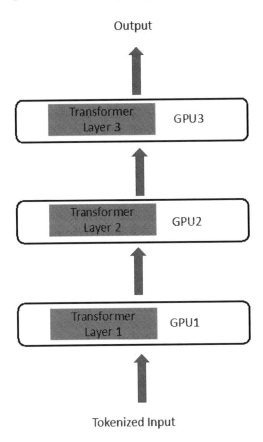

Figure 8.1 – Simplified illustration of a three-layer language model

As shown in the preceding diagram, we assume the input data has already been tokenized and can be directly fed into the model for either model training or model serving stages. We have a three-layer model. Each layer is an independent transformer layer, and each single transformer layer is allocated on a separate GPU.

Now, let's discuss how to freeze fully trained layers during the model training. We'll first describe how model freezing works during forward propagation. After that, we will cover how to reduce computation costs by freezing layers during backward propagation.

Freezing layers during forward propagation

During regular forward propagation, we need to calculate intermediate results per layer, such as activations/feature maps. Thus, for each layer, we need to do the following two things:

1. Calculate intermediate results for the current layer.

2. Send out the layer output to the successive GPU.

A detailed illustration of the preceding two steps is shown in the following diagram:

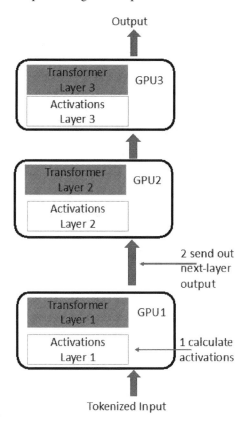

Figure 8.2 – Generating activation and propagating layer outputs during forward propagation

As shown in the preceding diagram, for each layer, we need to calculate its local activations (activation 1 in layer 1) that need computation resources. In addition, we need to hold the activations within each GPU's local memory, which also introduces memory consumption.

Now, let's assume that after several training iterations, layer 1 first converged, and we want to freeze layer 1.

The first thing we can do is to reduce the memory consumption for holding layer 1's activations. As shown in *Figure 8.3*, after we generate the output for the next layer, we can abandon the local activations for layer 1.

The whole layer 1 freezing works in the following three steps:

1.   Generates activations during forward propagation (same as regular training)
2.   Generates layer output to layer 2 (same as regular training)
3.   Deletes local activations (new)

Therefore, by freezing layer 1 during forward propagation, we can reduce the on-device memory consumption by deleting the layer's local activations. It is shown as the shaded box in the following diagram:

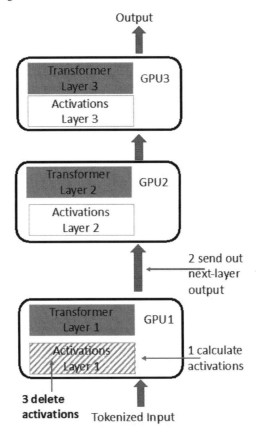

Figure 8.3 – Reducing memory consumption of the freezing layer 1

As shown in the preceding diagram, we just add *Step 3* (bottom-left corner) in order to delete layer 1's local activations.

In this section, we have discussed how to reduce GPU memory consumption by deleting the activations on the freezing layers during model forward propagation. Next, we will discuss how to reduce the computation cost of freezing layers during forward propagation.

Reducing computation cost during forward propagation

Since we reduced memory consumption for the freezing layers, we can leverage the memory we saved for data caching. Given that we train the model using the same input dataset, each data item will be repeated, passing into the model during the training session. Therefore, we can maintain a data cache, as shown in the following diagram:

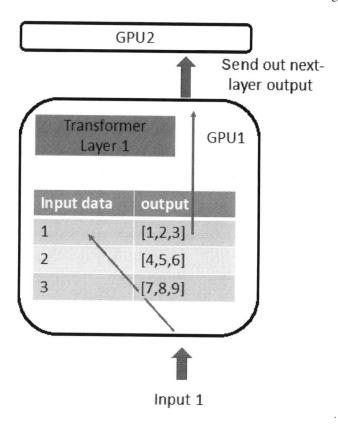

Figure 8.4 – Maintaining input/output (I/O) mapping cache inside GPU memory of the freezing layer

As shown in the preceding diagram, suppose our training dataset consists of three different training input data items. During the first round of training over the whole dataset, we cache the input data **identifier** (**ID**) and its corresponding next-layer output inside the GPU memory.

Next time the same training input data is fed into the GPU, we do not need to calculate its corresponding output again. Instead, we can directly read the output from the mapping cache we saved during the first training round.

For example, in *Figure 8.4*, if we see that training input 1 is fed into the GPU, we conduct the following steps:

1. We search over our mapping cache to see whether input 1 exists.
2. If it exists, we directly read its corresponding output from our cache.
3. We directly send out the corresponding output without repeatedly calculating it over and over again.

If the training data is not maintained in our cache, we calculate its corresponding output, then add the (input id, output) tuple into our cache.

By following the preceding steps, we achieve these benefits:

- Reduce the memory consumption for holding activations of the freezing layer inside the GPU.
- Avoid recomputation during forward propagation when encountering the same input data during training.

Next, we will discuss our optimization during the backward propagation of the freezing layers.

Freezing layers during backward propagation

As we did in the preceding forward propagation section, here, we will first illustrate what the steps are during regular backward propagation on the language model. A detailed illustration is depicted here:

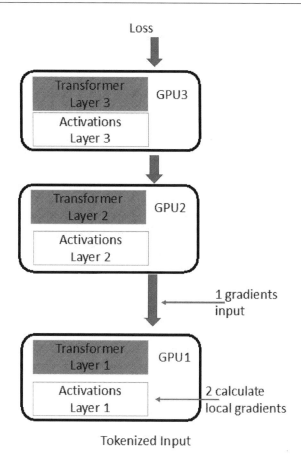

Figure 8.5 – Regular backward propagation of NLP model fine-tuning

As shown in the preceding diagram, during backward propagation of the NLP model at the fine-tuning stage, we first need to calculate loss (at the top).

After that, we backpropagate the gradients from **GPU3** to **GPU2** to **GPU1**. Basically, for each GPU, it conducts local gradient computation in the following three steps:

1. Receives the gradients' input from the previous GPU
2. Calculates local gradients using both the gradients' input of the previous GPU and their local activation values
3. Outputs the gradients to the next GPU

Now, let's still assume the layer we can freeze is layer 1. Therefore, for the backward propagation, we do not need to compute the gradients on **GPU1** anymore, which saves a lot of computation power. Computing gradients is usually more computationally expensive than calculating activations during forward propagation.

A detailed illustration of freezing layer 1 during backward propagation is provided here:

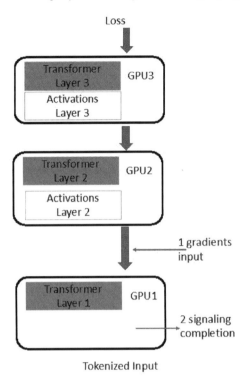

Figure 8.6 – Operations of freezing layer (layer 1) during backward propagation

As shown in the preceding diagram, we mentioned that we abandon the activation during the forward propagation on layer 1. Thus, there is no *activation layer 1* inside **GPU1**.

During the backward propagation, the freezing layer 1 on **GPU1** works as follows:

1. Receives the gradients' input from **GPU2**.
2. After completely receiving gradients from **GPU2**, **GPU1** signals to the job scheduler that current backward propagation has been completed.

With the preceding two steps, we skip the backward propagation on **GPU1**, which is normally very computationally intensive. Furthermore, since we ignore the backward propagation on **GPU1**, we also save time calculating gradients on **GPU1**. Thus, we shrink down the overall training time per iteration.

It is commonly believed that using layer-freezing techniques may hurt the model performance regarding test accuracy. Thus, in the next section, we will explore other techniques that can improve system efficiency during model-parallel training and inference.

Exploring memory and storage resources

In this section, we will discuss another way to improve system throughput during model-parallel training and inference.

One big limitation for GPU-based DNN training is the on-device memory size. In this section, we will extend the GPU training memory size by leveraging other storage within the system, such as CPU memory, hard drive, and more.

Before we jump into our techniques, let's see the interconnection between the CPU, GPU, and disk, as shown in the following diagram:

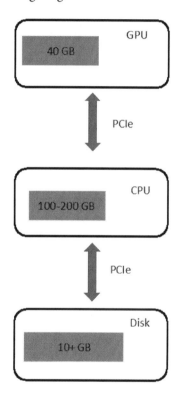

Figure 8.7 – System layout within a single machine

As shown in the preceding diagram, with SOTA hardware machines such as NVIDIA DGX-1 and DGX-2, the storage specifications are as follows:

- The GPU memory is usually around 40 **gigabytes** (**GB**).

- The CPU memory (main memory) is around hundreds of GB (for example, 100 GB-200 GB).

- The disk storage is around tens of **terabytes** (**TB**).

On the connection side, both the GPU and disk are connected with the CPU via a PCIe bus, which can give you around 10-15 **GB per second (GB/s)** data transfer speed.

As shown in *Figure 8.7*, both CPU memory and disk storage are much bigger than GPU memory size. Therefore, if the GPU memory is not sufficient for maintaining some intermediate results during DNN model training, we can move it to the CPU memory or disk. When we need to use those data chunks, we can prefetch them back to GPU memory from CPU memory or disk.

We can follow two directions to leverage CPU memory and disk storage: save and load. The first is to save data to CPU memory or disk, while the second is to load data back to GPU memory. For saving data to CPU memory or disk, the data being saved can follow the data pipeline shown in the following diagram:

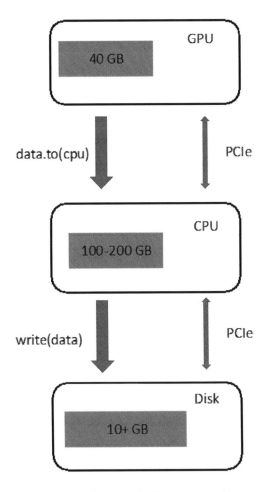

Figure 8.8 – Saving data into CPU memory or disk storage

As shown in the preceding diagram, we can easily convert GPU/**Compute Unified Device Architecture (CUDA)** tensors to CPU tensors by using a function call such as the `data.to(cpu)` function. If CPU memory is not enough, we can further move data from CPU memory to disk with file write function calls such as `write(data)` to the disk's filesystem.

To sum up, to save more intermediate results on the GPU, we do the following operations:

1. Move data from GPU memory to CPU memory by calling `data.to(cpu)`.
2. Synchronize on this data-move function call and wait for it to finish.
3. If CPU memory is not big enough, let the CPU write data to disk storage by calling file write function calls such as `write(data)`.
4. Synchronize on the file writing process and wait for it to finish.

Similarly, once we want to read the external data back to GPU memory, we can carry out the instructions shown in the following diagram. Basically, it is the inverse direction of data transfer shown in *Figure 8.8*:

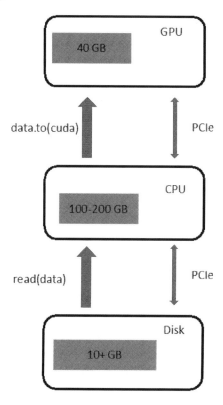

Figure 8.9 – Loading data back to GPU memory from CPU memory or disk storage

In a nutshell, to load data from disk/CPU memory to GPU memory, we need to carry out the following operations:

1. If data is on disk storage, we first let the CPU run file read functions such as `read(data)` to load data from disk to CPU memory.

2. Synchronize and wait for the data transfer from disk to CPU memory to finish.

3. Then, start converting the data format from CPU to GPU and transfer data from CPU memory to GPU memory.

4. Synchronize and wait for the data transfer from CPU to GPU memory to finish.

With the preceding data transfer scheme shown in both *Figure 8.8* and *Figure 8.9*, we can further extend the GPU memory size to the CPU memory size or even the disk size.

In addition, to further speed up this data transfer process, we can adopt some techniques that were used in traditional operating systems, such as **data prefetching**. Thus, before the GPU really wants to use the data, it tries to prefetch the data. Then, the GPU can do computation over the data when needed without waiting for the data transfer time.

Next, we will discuss a third optimization scheme that tries to split the giant model into small pieces without communication in between.

Understanding model decomposition and distillation

The third technique we introduce here is called **model decomposition and distillation**.

At a high level, model decomposition tries to split the giant model into small subnets and thus minimize the communication among those subnets.

For each DNN, we will further reduce its size by performing model pruning, which is also called **model distillation**.

Now, we will talk about each technique in detail.

Model decomposition

One SOTA approach for model decomposition is sensAI, which can almost eliminate communication among the subnets split from the giant base model. Basically, we assume we have a fully trained model.

For the ease of illustration, we assume the DNN base model here is just a **convolutional neural network (CNN)** and the fully trained base model is used for image classification between cats and dogs.

The following diagram depicts how we split this model into disconnected subnets:

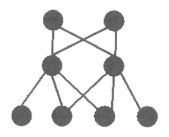

Base model

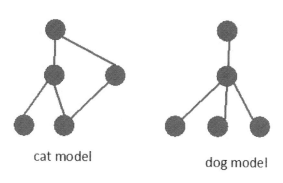

cat model   dog model

Figure 8.10 – Model decomposition is used to remove communication

As shown in the preceding diagram, we split the base model into two subnets, given that the base model (at the top of *Figure 8.10*) can classify both cat and dog images. After the model split, each of the subnets (at the bottom of *Figure 8.10*) can only classify either cat or dog images.

Therefore, by doing this divide-and-conquer model split, there is zero communication needed among all these subnets during both model training and model serving stages. The attribute of zero communication is really important because, in traditional model parallelism, a lot of time is wasted due to cross-GPU communication. Eliminating communication among all the model partitions in model parallelism can significantly improve both model-parallel training and serving speed.

In order to achieve this zero-communication version of model parallelism, we need to follow the next steps, which are also depicted in *Figure 8.11*:

1. We assume we have a fully trained base model.

2. We pass in the training data per one class (dog) into the fully trained base model, then collect the neurons that are fired up.

3. We pull out those fired neurons and form a smaller subnet for this particular class (dog).

Let's take a look at the diagram now:

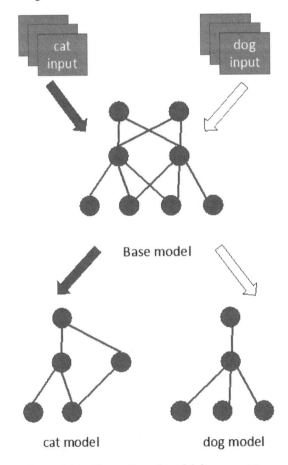

Figure 8.11 – Illustration of model decomposition

As shown in the preceding diagram, by following the preceding steps, we can split the base model into two separate cat and dog subnets. Thus, the zero-communication model split finishes.

Model distillation

Model distillation is orthogonal to the model decomposition scheme we mentioned earlier. In general, given any model, model distillation tries to prune redundant neurons from the model. Thus, by adopting model distillation, we can further shrink down the model sizes.

A simple illustration is shown here:

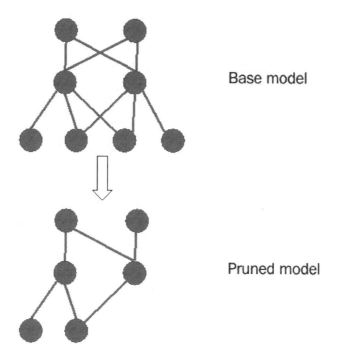

Figure 8.12 – Model distillation via pruning

As shown in *Figure 8.12*, we define some model-pruning criteria. Then, we determine whether to prune the neuron or not based on these pre-defined pruning criteria.

After the pruning step, we can get a much smaller model while maintaining the same functionality.

Reducing bits in hardware

A recent study shows that using fewer bits to represent model weights will not introduce significant model test accuracy. Given this observation, we can use fewer bits to represent each weight value inside a DNN model. A simple example is shown here:

Figure 8.13 – Reducing bit representation per model weight

As shown in *Figure 8.13*, we can reduce the bit representation from **FP32** to **FP16**. We can further reduce the bits by moving from **FP16** to **INT8**.

Summary

In this chapter, we mainly discussed how to improve system efficiency in model-parallel training and serving.

After reading this chapter, you should be able to freeze some layers during model-parallel training. In addition, you can also use CPU memory or disk as the GPU's external data storage. Furthermore, you should have also mastered techniques such as model decomposition, model distillation, and reduced bit representation.

In the next chapter, we will discuss advanced techniques such as combining data parallelism and model parallelism.

Section 3 – Advanced Parallelism Paradigms

In this section, we will learn state-of-the-art techniques on top of traditional data and model parallelism approaches. First, we will understand the concept of hybrid data-model parallelism. Second, we will discuss federated learning and edge device learning. Third, we will discuss elastic and in-parallel model training/inference in multitenant clusters or cloud environments. Finally, we will look at some more advanced techniques for further accelerating in-parallel model training and serving.

This section comprises the following chapters:

- *Chapter 9, A Hybrid of Data and Model Parallelism*
- *Chapter 10, Federated Learning and Edge Devices*
- *Chapter 11, Elastic Model Training and Serving*
- *Chapter 12, Advanced Techniques for Further Speed-Ups*

9

A Hybrid of Data and Model Parallelism

In general, we have two different parallelism schemes—data parallelism and model parallelism. Each of them has advantages and disadvantages. In this chapter, we will try to leverage both data parallelism and model parallelism together. We call it a **hybrid of data parallelism and model parallelism**.

Before we discuss this further, we want to list our assumptions, as follows:

- Even though the advanced **graphics processing unit** (**GPU**) from NVIDIA now supports **multi-tenancy**, we still assume that one job occupies the whole GPU.

- When our training or serving job starts running, we do not allow job preemption or system interruption.

- We assume the use of homogenous GPUs for a single job.

- We assume the interconnects between GPUs within a machine are **NVLink** or **NVSwitch**.

- We assume the links among different machines use **traditional Ethernet** or **InfiniBand** (**IB**).

- We assume **intra-machine communication bandwidth** is higher compared to **inter-machine communication bandwidth**.

- We assume we have enough GPUs for running a **deep neural network (DNN)** model training or model serving job.

- Our approach can be generally applied to other hardware accelerators such as **tensor processing units (TPUs)** and **field-programmable gate arrays (FPGAs)**. However, we limit our discussion to GPU-based DNN training or serving workloads.

In this chapter, we mainly focus on two **state-of-the-art (SOTA)** techniques that use both data parallelism and model parallelism. For this hybrid parallelism scheme, we'll do a case study on two specific systems: **Megatron-LM** from *NVIDIA* and **Mesh-TensorFlow** from *Google*. Both are widely used in industry and academia.

First, we will discuss the techniques used in Megatron-LM and how it achieves hybrid data parallelism and model parallelism. Second, we will briefly discuss how to use Megatron-LM. For more details on using Megatron-LM, we will list the official website of their user manuals. Third, we will discuss the core ideas of Mesh-TensorFlow and how it leverages both data and model parallelism. Fourth, we will also briefly mention how to use Mesh-TensorFlow and attach useful links to Mesh-TensorFlow's official user manuals. Finally, we will discuss the pros and cons of using both systems.

In a nutshell, you will cover the following topics in this chapter:

- Case study of Megatron-LM

- Implementation of Megatron-LM

- Case study of Mesh-TensorFlow

- Implementation of Mesh-TensorFlow

- Pros and cons of Megatron-LM and Mesh-TensorFlow

Now, we will first look at how Megatron-LM works in general, then we will talk about how to use Megatron-LM for DNN training. After that, we will discuss Mesh-TensorFlow and summarize the chapter.

Technical requirements

We assume the use of both PyTorch and TensorFlow for our implementation platform. The main library dependencies for our code are listed as follows:

- `torch` >= 1.7.1
- `tensorflow` >= 2.6
- `mesh-tensorflow` >= 0.0.5
- `pip` > 19.0 (Ubuntu)
- `pip` > 20.3 (macOS)
- `numpy` >= 1.19.0
- `python` >= 3.7
- `ubuntu` >= 16.04
- `transformers` >= 4.10.3
- `cuda` >= 11.0
- `torchvision` >= 0.10.0
- NVIDIA driver >= 450.119.03

It is mandatory to have the preceding libraries pre-installed with the correct versions.

Case study of Megatron-LM

Megatron-LM is a large-scale DNN training system developed at NVIDIA. It uses data parallelism and model parallelism together.

Let's first talk about how Megatron-LM splits models using model parallelism. Then, we will discuss how it is extended to use data parallelism as well.

Layer split for model parallelism

We will first illustrate how Megatron-LM uses model parallelism within a multi-GPU machine. Let's focus on a simple matrix multiplication case.

General Matrix Multiply (GEMM) is widely used in the DNN layers of language models.

Suppose we have matrix A, as shown in the following diagram:

A(0,0)	A(0,1)	A(0,2)	A(0,3)
A(1,0)	A(1,1)	A(1,2)	A(1,3)
A(2,0)	A(2,1)	A(2,2)	A(2,3)
A(3,0)	A(3,1)	A(3,2)	A(3,3)

Matrix A

(weights)

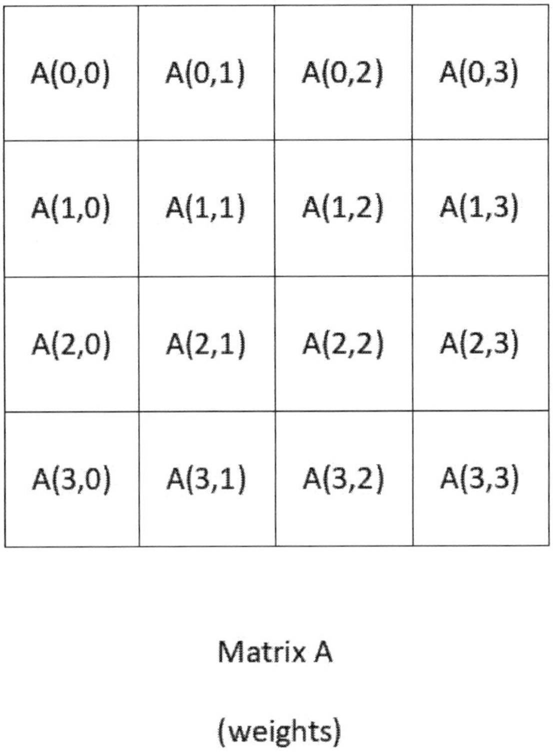

Figure 9.1 – Weight matrix of a layer in a language model

As shown in the preceding diagram, for one particular layer of a language model, we have a **weight matrix**. We call the weight matrix A. A is a 4x4 weight matrix.

Now, let's assume we have some input data for this DNN layer. We call the input data X. Therefore, what we want to do is $X*A$, which is shown in the following diagram:

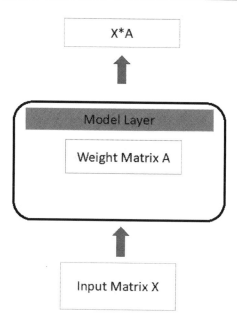

Figure 9.2 – Matrix multiplication between weights and input (X*A)

As shown in *Figure 9.2*, given input X and weight matrix A, we want to output $X*A$.

Now, let's assume the X matrix is in the following format:

X(0,0)	X(0,1)	X(0,2)	X(0,3)
X(1,0)	X(1,1)	X(1,2)	X(1,3)
X(2,0)	X(2,1)	X(2,2)	X(2,3)
X(3,0)	X(3,1)	X(3,2)	X(3,3)

Matrix X

(Input)

Figure 9.3 – Input matrix X

As shown in *Figure 9.3*, we assume we have input matrix *X* in the shape of 4x4. Note that in a real-world application, the *X* matrix shape does not need to match the shape of an *A* matrix. This layer-input split method can be directly applied to cases with which matrix *A* and *X* shapes do not match.

After we calculate *X*A*, we want to apply some non-linear function on top of this result. Basically, the final output we want is *y*, as follows:

$$y \ = \ ReLU(X * A)$$

We'll now illustrate how Megatron-LM splits both input matrix *X* and weight matrix *A* separately.

Row-wise trial-and-error approach

Let's try a trial-and-error approach. Let's first try to split both input matrix *X* and weight matrix *A*.

First, we split weight matrix *A* along its rows, as shown in the following diagram:

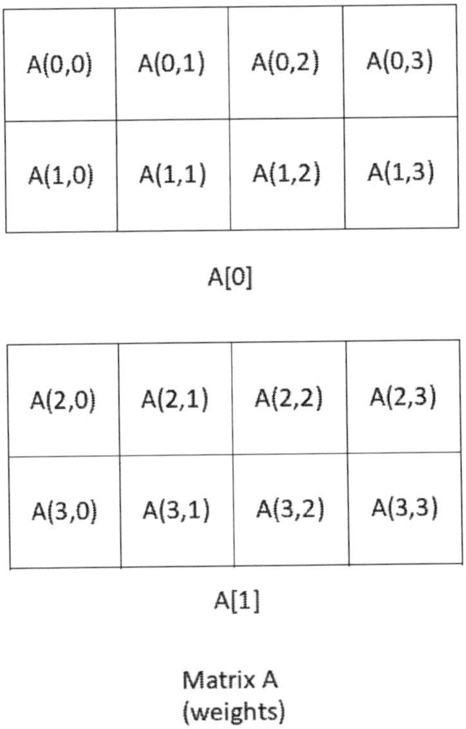

A(0,0)	A(0,1)	A(0,2)	A(0,3)
A(1,0)	A(1,1)	A(1,2)	A(1,3)

A[0]

A(2,0)	A(2,1)	A(2,2)	A(2,3)
A(3,0)	A(3,1)	A(3,2)	A(3,3)

A[1]

Matrix A
(weights)

Figure 9.4 – Row-wise split of weight matrix A

As shown in the preceding diagram, we split weight matrix A along its rows—that is, between row *[1]* and row *[2]*. So, matrix A is split into two parts, as follows:

- *A[0]* contains row *[0,1]*.
- *A[1]* contains row *[2,3]*.

Next, let's try to split input matrix X along its columns.

Basically, given input matrix X, we want to group the first half of the columns together and then the second half of the columns together, as shown in the following diagram:

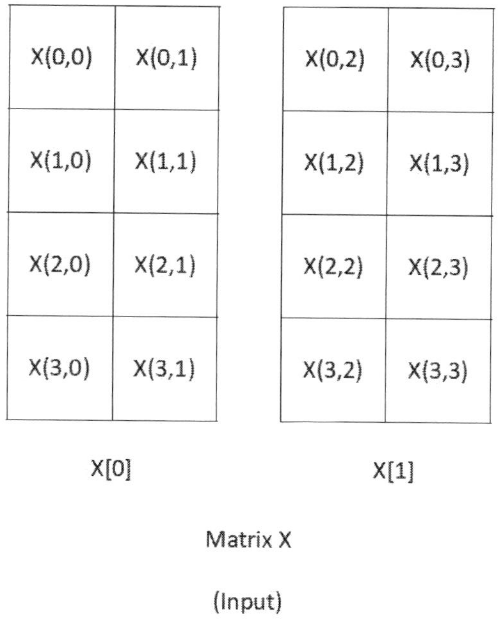

X(0,0)	X(0,1)
X(1,0)	X(1,1)
X(2,0)	X(2,1)
X(3,0)	X(3,1)

X[0]

X(0,2)	X(0,3)
X(1,2)	X(1,3)
X(2,2)	X(2,3)
X(3,2)	X(3,3)

X[1]

Matrix X

(Input)

Figure 9.5 – Input matrix X split along columns

As shown in the preceding diagram, we split input matrix X into two parts along its columns, as follows:

- *X[0]* contains column *[0][1]*.
- *X[1]* contains column *[2][3]*.

After we split both input matrix X and weight matrix A, we can now do the matrix multiplication among these split pieces in parallel.

First, we will calculate the first part as follows:

$$X[0] * A[0]$$

The following diagram shows which parts of X and A are paired together:

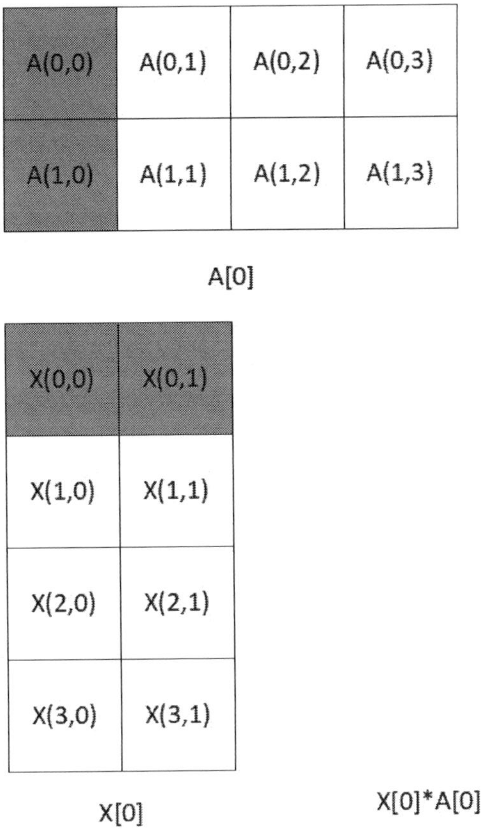

A(0,0)	A(0,1)	A(0,2)	A(0,3)
A(1,0)	A(1,1)	A(1,2)	A(1,3)

A[0]

X(0,0)	X(0,1)
X(1,0)	X(1,1)
X(2,0)	X(2,1)
X(3,0)	X(3,1)

X[0]   X[0]*A[0]

Figure 9.6 – Matrix multiplication of X[0] and A[0]

The matrix multiplication of the first half of X and the first half of A is depicted in the preceding diagram. Basically, we multiply each column of matrix A[0] with each row of matrix X[0].

The multiplication between the first column of A[0] and the first row of X[0] is denoted with gray boxes in *Figure 9.6*.

Similarly, we can conduct the same matrix multiplication on A[1] and X[1], as follows:

$$X[1] * A[1]$$

This detailed operation is depicted here:

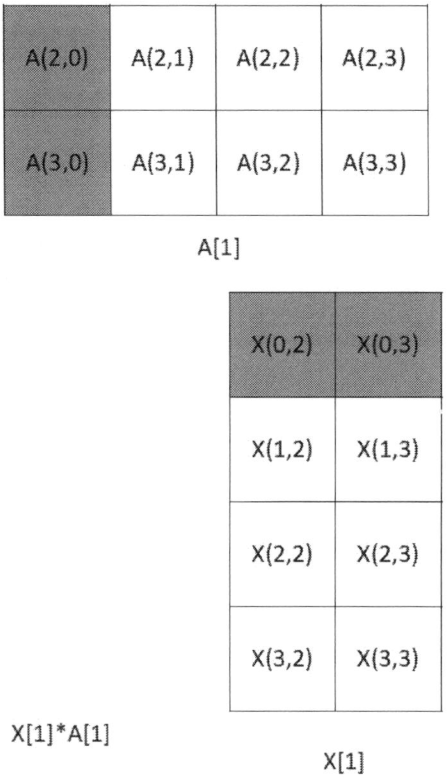

| A(2,0) | A(2,1) | A(2,2) | A(2,3) |
| A(3,0) | A(3,1) | A(3,2) | A(3,3) |

A[1]

X(0,2)	X(0,3)
X(1,2)	X(1,3)
X(2,2)	X(2,3)
X(3,2)	X(3,3)

X[1]*A[1]

X[1]

Figure 9.7 – Second-half GEMM between X[1] and A[1]

As shown in *Figure 9.7*, we conduct similar matrix multiplication on the second half of both input matrix *X[1]* and weight matrix *A[1]*.

The first matrix multiplication operation is shown as gray boxes in *Figure 9.7*. It shows the matrix multiplication of the first row in *X[1]* and the first column in *A[1]*.

So far, it seems OK to split the matrix multiplication in the preceding way. However, as we mentioned, we may want to apply some non-linear function on top of matrix multiplication results, as follows:

$$y = ReLU(XA)$$

Now, we may have some problems given our split implementation because, after our matrix split, we have the following result:

$$X[0] * A[0]$$

We also have this result:

$$X[1] * A[1]$$

However, if we want to apply the ReLU non-linear function on top of these matrix multiplication results, we get the following:

$$y' = ReLU(X[0] * A[0]) + ReLU(X[1] * A[1])$$

Given the definition of the non-linear function, we can conclude the following outcome:

$$y! = y'$$

Therefore, our trial-and-error approach illustrated previously may not work if we have a non-linear function in the end. Thus, we may want to find some other matrix-split scheme.

Column-wise trial-and-error approach

For the second trial-and-error approach, we try to split the weight matrix along its column dimension, as shown here:

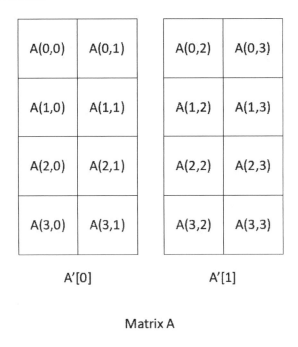

Matrix A

(weights)

Figure 9.8 – Split weight matrix along its columns

As shown in the preceding diagram, we try to split weight matrix *A* along its columns rather than its rows. After the split, we can get the following:

- *A'[0]* contains column *[0]* and column *[1]*.
- *A'[1]* contains column *[2]* and column *[3]*.

In this approach, we do not split the input *X* matrix because if we allocate *A'[0]* and *A'[1]* on two different GPUs, we can share the *X* matrix by duplicating it on both GPUs.

Now, we will illustrate how to do matrix multiplication in this setting. We will perform the following actions:

- Split weight matrix *A* in the column dimension.
- Do not split input matrix *X*.

The first half of the matrix multiplication is shown here:

$$X * A'[0]$$

We highlight the computation as darker boxes here:

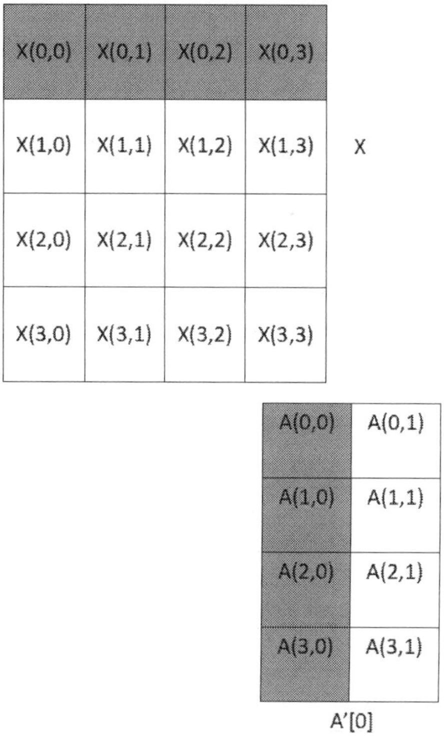

X(0,0)	X(0,1)	X(0,2)	X(0,3)
X(1,0)	X(1,1)	X(1,2)	X(1,3)
X(2,0)	X(2,1)	X(2,2)	X(2,3)
X(3,0)	X(3,1)	X(3,2)	X(3,3)

X

A(0,0)	A(0,1)
A(1,0)	A(1,1)
A(2,0)	A(2,1)
A(3,0)	A(3,1)

A'[0]

Figure 9.9 – Matrix multiplication of X and A'[0]

As shown in the preceding diagram, we can directly apply matrix multiplication on X and $A'[0]$. The first matrix multiplication pair is shown as gray boxes in *Figure 9.9*. Basically, we will multiply matrices of row 0 of X and column 0 of $A'[0]$.

Similarly, we can apply another matrix multiplication on the second half of A as $A'[1]$.

Given $A'[1]$, we want to do the following:

$$X * A'[1]$$

This operation is depicted in the following diagram:

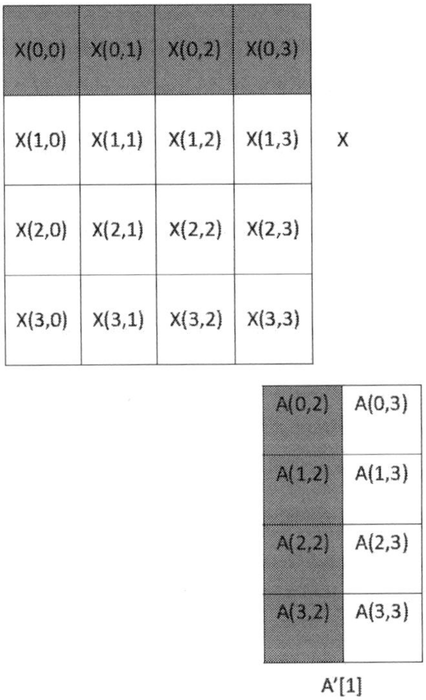

X(0,0)	X(0,1)	X(0,2)	X(0,3)
X(1,0)	X(1,1)	X(1,2)	X(1,3)
X(2,0)	X(2,1)	X(2,2)	X(2,3)
X(3,0)	X(3,1)	X(3,2)	X(3,3)

X

A(0,2)	A(0,3)
A(1,2)	A(1,3)
A(2,2)	A(2,3)
A(3,2)	A(3,3)

A'[1]

Figure 9.10 – Matrix multiplication of X and A'[1]

As shown in the preceding diagram, we can calculate the second half-matrix multiplication between X and $A'[1]$.

We get two partially multiplied results. Here's the first one:

$$X * A'[0]$$

And here's the second one:

$$X * A'[1]$$

Now, let's discuss how to add the ReLU non-linear function on top.

Here, we apply the ReLU function on top of the preceding matrix multiplication results and get the following result:

$$y'' = ReLU(X * A'[0], X * A'[1])$$
$$= [ReLU(X * A'[0]), ReLU(X * A'[1])]$$

The original output value we want is this:

$$y = ReLU(X * A)$$

Now, you can see the following:

$$y = y''$$

Thus, this layer-weight split works.

Basically, this is what Megatron-LM does for intra-layer model splitting. For gradient calculations and some **batch normalization** (**batch norm**) calculations, Megatron-LM will inject an additional identity matrix or an AllReduce function to guarantee that this layer split has the exact same functionality as the non-split version of DNN training.

Therefore, Megatron-LM can split the model into two dimensions, as follows:

- The first dimension is a layer-wise split.

- The second dimension is a weight-matrix split within a layer.

A more detailed model split is shown in the following diagram:

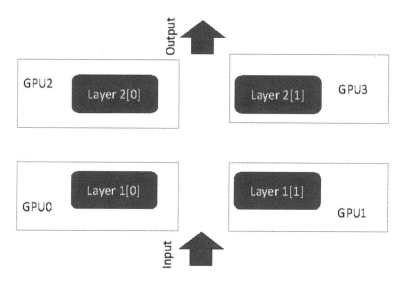

Figure 9.11 – Simplified model split in Megatron-LM

As shown in the preceding diagram, we assume we have a two-layer language model. Given two model split dimensions in Megatron-LM, we can split this two-layer model into four GPUs. The model split is outlined as follows:

- *GPU0* contains the first half of layer 1 as *Layer 1[0]*.

- *GPU1* contains the second half of layer 1 as *Layer 1[1]*.

- *GPU2* contains the first half of layer 2 as *Layer 2[0]*.

- *GPU3* contains the second half of layer 2 as *Layer 2[1]*.

Therefore, by achieving an intra-layer split and an inter-layer split, Megatron-LM can split a single model into multiple GPUs in a very efficient way.

Next, we will discuss how to add data parallelism on top of Megatron-LM's model parallelism.

Cross-machine for data parallelism

At a high level, Megatron-LM combines data parallelism with model parallelism in a hierarchy. This process works on two levels, as follows:

- For multiple GPUs within a machine, Megatron conducts model parallelism as shown in *Figure 9.11*.

- For cross-machine cases, Megatron-LM uses data parallelism to enable concurrent training on different input batches.

Since model parallelism within a machine is depicted in *Figure 9.11*, we'll just focus on how to do cross-machine data parallelism in Megatron-LM.

Megatron-LM's hybrid data model parallelism is shown in the following diagram:

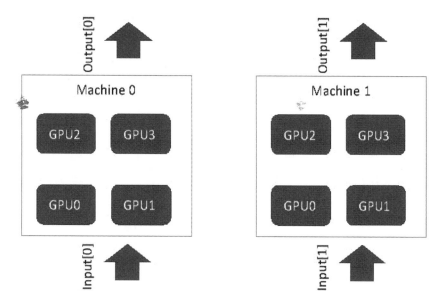

Figure 9.12 – Megatron-LM's hybrid data model parallelism

As shown in the preceding diagram, Megatron-LM achieves data parallelism in cross-machine cases. Here, suppose we have two four-GPU machines. Thus, Megatron-LM conducts model-parallel training on the four GPUs within the two machines and then conducts data parallel training between the two machines.

By building this training hierarchy, Megatron-LM can achieve both data parallelism and model parallelism simultaneously.

Implementation of Megatron-LM

In this section, we will briefly discuss how to use Megatron-LM. For more details, you can read the official user manual of Megatron-LM here: `https://github.com/NVIDIA/Megatron-LM`. Here are the steps we need to follow:

1. To use Megatron-LM, we first need to install some pre-trained checkpoints, as follows:

```
# Download checkpoints
# Terminal

wget --content-disposition \
    models/nvidia/megatron_lm_345m/ \
    versions/ \
```

```
        v0.1/zip \
        -0 \
        megatron_lm_345m_v0.1.zip
```

2. After that, you can use megatron-lm to preprocess the data, as follows:

```
# pre-process data

python3 preprocess_data.py \
        --input xxx.json \
        --output-prefix my-model \
        --vocab bert-vercab.txt \
        --dataset-impl mmap \
        --split-sentences
```

3. Then, you can do the pre-training, as follows:

```
# Bert pre-training

Checkpoint_path = checkpoint/bert_model

Vocab = bert-vocab.txt
Data_path = bert-text-sentence

Bert_args = --num_layer = 12 \
        --hidden_size = 512 \
        --lr = 0.01 \
        --epoch = 1000000 \
        --lr-decay = 990000 \
        --seq-length = 256 \
        --split 50,50,2 \
        -- min-lr = 0.00001 \
        --fp32
. . .
output_args= --log-interval 100 \
        --eval-iter 50 \
        --save-interval 300
. . .
```

```
python3 pretrain_bert.py \
     $Bert_args \
     $output_args \
     --save_path $checkpoint_path
. . .
```

By applying the preceding setup and running the `pretrain_bert.py` file, we can start using Megatron-LM for model training of **Bidirectional Encoder Representations from Transformers (BERT)**. For more details, you can read their user manual by going to the link posted at the beginning of this section.

Case study of Mesh-TensorFlow

We discussed Megatron-LM in detail due to its popularity. Now, we will briefly discuss Mesh-TensorFlow in this section.

This approach is quite easy to understand. Basically, Mesh-TensorFlow combines data and model parallelism by allowing users to configure two dimensions—that is, batch and model dimensions—as shown in the following diagram:

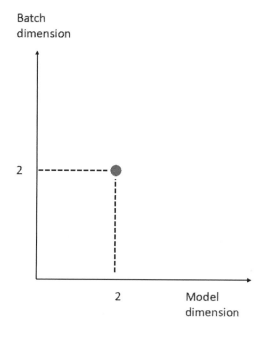

Figure 9.13 – Mesh-TensorFlow's two-dimensional (2D) parallelism

As shown in the preceding diagram, `mesh-tensorflow` allows users to set parallelism levels in two dimensions, as follows:

- **Batch dimension**: How many concurrent batches to train (data parallelism)
- **Model dimension**: How many splits over the model (model parallelism)

As shown in *Figure 9.13*, let's assume the user sets both batch dimension as **2** and model dimension as **2**. This means that we use two GPUs to do model-parallel training, and we have two groups of this two-GPU model parallelism. Among these two groups, we do data parallel training.

Since Megatron-LM is a more popular solution, we just briefly discussed `mesh-tensorflow` here. Next, we will also talk about implementation using `mesh-tensorflow`.

Implementation of Mesh-TensorFlow

A detailed user manual for `mesh-tensorflow` can be found here: `https://github.com/tensorflow/mesh`.

To use `mesh-tensorflow`, you first need to install it, as follows:

```
# installation
#first step
pip3 install tensorflow
# GPU support
pip3 install tensorflow-gpu
#second step
pip3 install mesh-tensorflow
```

After that, you can use `mesh-tensorflow` directly for distributed tensor operations.

Pros and cons of Megatron-LM and Mesh-TensorFlow

Now, we will briefly discuss the pros and cons of Megatron-LM and Mesh-TensorFlow.

In general, Mesh-TensorFlow is built on top of TensorFlow, which is not very popular when compared with PyTorch-based solutions. The most important thing is that TensorFlow code is more complicated to write when compared with PyTorch.

From a research standpoint, Mesh-TensorFlow does not involve significant research when compared with Megatron-LM.

Therefore, in a nutshell, we suggest that you use Megatron-LM.

Summary

In this chapter, we discussed advanced techniques on a hybrid of data parallelism and model parallelism. Next, we did a case study of Megatron-LM and its implementation, followed by a case study of Mesh-TensorFlow and its implementation. We ended the chapter by learning about the pros and cons of the two systems.

After reading this chapter, you should understand how Megatron-LM achieves both model parallelism and data parallelism simultaneously. You should be able to use Megatron-LM to launch your own DNN model training job. In addition, you should be familiar with the high-level idea of Mesh-TensorFlow and how to use it for model training as well.

In the next chapter, we will discuss federated learning.

10
Federated Learning and Edge Devices

When discussing DNN training, we mainly focus on using high-performance computers with accelerators such as GPUs or traditional data centers. Federated learning takes a different approach, trying to train models on edge devices, which usually have much less computation power compared with GPUs.

Before we discuss anything further, we want to list our assumptions:

- We assume the computation power of mobile chips is much less than traditional hardware accelerators such as GPUs/TPUs.

- We assume mobile devices often have a limited computation budget due to the limited battery power.

- We assume the model training/serving platform for a mobile device will be different from the model training/serving platform for data centers.

- We assume users are not willing to directly share their local personal data with the service provider.

- We assume the communication bandwidth between mobile devices and the service provider is limited.

- We assume there may be high latency or data loss during the communication between servers and mobile devices.

- We assume a mobile device may shut down due to a power outage.

- We assume the DNN training/serving platform can run successfully without any system capability issues.

- During DNN training, we assume the user may have false-positive and false-negative samples.

In this chapter, we discuss a new distributed DNN training and serving paradigm, which is called **federated learning**. At a high level, federated learning refers to using millions of mobile phones to collectively train and revise a DNN model in a fully distributed manner.

First, we will discuss the basic concepts of federated learning and its application scenarios. Second, we will illustrate how it works by conducting a case study over the TensorFlow Federated platform. Third, we will introduce how edge devices conduct tiny model training and serving with TinyML. Finally, we will conduct a case study over TensorFlow Lite, which is used for DNN model deployment on mobile devices and even simpler **internet of things (IOT)** devices.

After going through this chapter, you will understand how federated learning works, and how it is different from our traditional DNN training/serving platform on data centers/GPUs. In addition, you will learn how to use TensorFlow Federated and TensorFlow Lite to train and deploy your tiny DNN models on your mobile phones or IoT devices.

In a nutshell, you will learn about the following topics going through this chapter:

- Sharing knowledge without sharing data
- Case study: TensorFlow Federated
- Running edge devices with TinyML
- Case study: TensorFlow Lite

Technical requirements

We'll use TensorFlow and its relevant platforms for our implementation platform. The main library dependencies for our code are illustrated as follows:

- `tensorflow>=2.6`
- `pip >19.0`
- `numpy>=1.19.0`
- `python>=3.7`
- `ubuntu>=16.04`
- `cuda>=11.0`
- `torchvision>=0.10.0`
- `Nvidia driver >=450.119.03`

It is mandatory to have the correct versions of the preceding libraries installed.

Sharing knowledge without sharing data

In this section, we will discuss the basic concepts of federated learning. For traditional distributed DNN training, each user/node can get global access to the whole training dataset. However, in federated learning, each user/node does not get global access to the whole training dataset. More specifically, federated learning enables distributed and collaborative training without sharing the input data.

We will first recap the traditional data parallel training. We will then discuss the main difference between traditional data parallel training and federated learning.

Recapping the traditional data parallel model training paradigm

Let's first look at a simple example of traditional data parallel training using parameter server architecture as shown in the following figure:

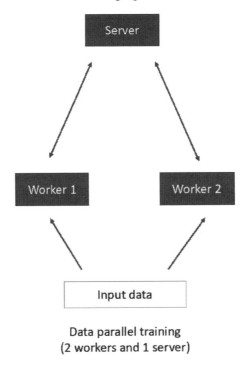

Data parallel training
(2 workers and 1 server)

Figure 10.1 – Normal data parallel training with two workers and one server

As shown in the preceding figure, in a normal data parallel training job, we use two machines/GPUs as two workers and we have one additional machine serving as a parameter server. Therefore, both **Worker 1** and **Worker 2** share the same input dataset. In other words, each of them has a global view of the whole input data. The only difference between **Worker 1** and **Worker 2** is each of them only pulls a dis-joint subset of the whole input data as their current training batch but both of them can access the whole dataset.

This simple parameter server architecture works by way of the following steps:

1. Each worker pulls some input data as the current training batch input.
2. Each worker trains its model locally.
3. Each worker submits its gradients to the parameter server.
4. The parameter server aggregates both workers' gradients.

5. The parameter server broadcasts the aggregated gradients to both workers.

6. The workers update their local model parameters.

During the whole training session, each worker/server loops over the preceding six steps until the model is converged.

Compared with traditional data parallel training, federated learning has the following two major differences:

- There is no local data sharing.

- Workers only communicate gradients.

Let's discuss each in turn.

No input sharing among workers

Let's first look at the first attribute of federated learning, which is to keep each user's local data private and to never communicate the local data.

Compared with traditional data parallel training, shown in *Figure 10.1*, a similar federated learning approach is shown in the following figure:

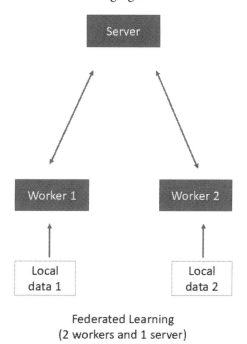

Federated Learning
(2 workers and 1 server)

Figure 10.2 – Federated learning with two workers and one server

As shown in the preceding figure, compared with data parallel training in *Figure 10.1*, each worker in federated learning maintains its own local data as **Local data 1** and **Local data 2** and these two workers never share their input data with each other.

Therefore, each machine can only use its own local data to carry out local model training. This local data training is not enough to train a good DNN model. The main reasons are as follows:

- Local data has high bias.
- The total size of local data is too small to train a DNN model.

If there is no synchronization with other nodes, the model trained on each worker may not be useful at all. Therefore, we need to figure out some communication scheme that shares local model information without exposing their local input data.

Communicating gradients for collaborative learning

To tackle the problem of sharing information without sharing input data, federated learning uses sharing knowledge. Sharing knowledge can be done in the following two ways:

- Sharing local model weights.
- Sharing local gradients.

One fact about the communication between servers and workers in federated learning is that it can often be choppy. Therefore, sharing local gradients after each training iteration may not be possible since some workers may not have access to the server for a long period of time. Therefore, sharing model weights seems to be a better choice.

In federated learning, the communication among workers and servers works as follows:

1. The server broadcasts the initial model weights to all the workers.
2. Each worker trains its local model with its own local data.
3. Each worker updates its local model weights.
4. The server collects the model weights from workers and then updates the global model weights.

The whole communication loops over the preceding four steps.

Let's first look at *step 1*, as shown in the following figure:

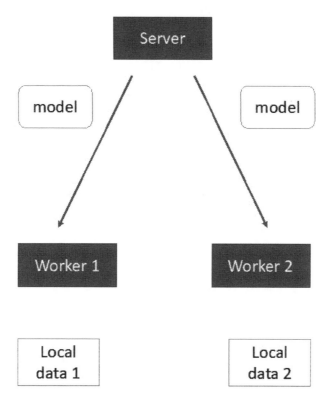

Figure 10.3 – The server broadcasts the DNN model to all the workers

As shown in the preceding figure, after the server decides which model to use, it initializes the model parameter and sends the model to all the workers in the system.

After each worker successfully receives the model, it will deploy the model locally on its own device and start preparing the local training data.

Next, we will discuss the communication, *step 2*, where each worker uses local data to train its model locally as depicted in the following figure:

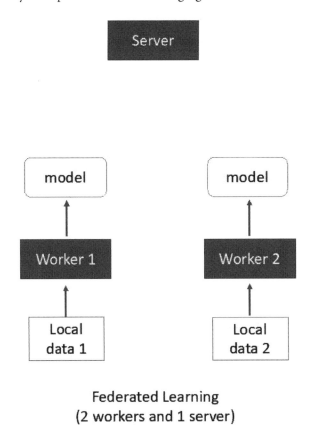

Figure 10.4 – Each worker using local data to train its local model

As shown in the preceding figure, after receiving the model from the server, each worker pulls its local dataset for local training.

For example, **Worker 1** does the following:

1.   It pulls **Local data 1** as the training input.

2.   It uses this local training data to train the model received from the server.

Worker 2 does the same thing.

After their local training iteration finishes, each of the workers will update its local model weights periodically as shown in the following figure:

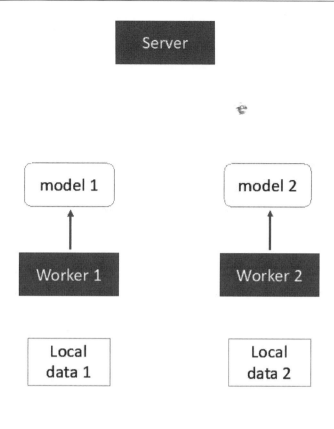

**Federated Learning
(2 workers and 1 server)**

Figure 10.5 – Local model updating on each worker

As shown in the preceding figure, after each worker uses its own local data to train its local model, it updates the base model with its own local gradients. Therefore, compared with the base model in *Figure 10.4*, now the models on each worker are different in *Figure 10.5*.

More specifically, as depicted in *Figure 10.5*, after each worker trains its local model and gets local gradients, it uses the local gradients to update its local model parameters. Since **Input data 1** and **Input data 2** are different, the updated model for **Worker 1** and **Worker 2** can be different. We call these different model versions **model 1** and **model 2**.

After each worker updates its local model weights, we come to step 4 of communication in federated learning, which is to let servers collect all the model versions and aggregate all of them. The whole process is shown in the following figure:

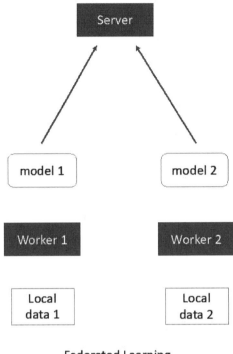

Federated Learning
(2 workers and 1 server)

Figure 10.6 – Server collecting all the local models from all workers

As shown in the preceding figure, after each worker generates its local models (such as **model 1** and **model 2** in *Figure 10.6*), the server will do the following:

1. The server collects all the models from all workers.

2. The server conducts the model aggregation. The model aggregation can be as simple as averaging all the model weights from all the workers.

3. The server broadcasts the aggregated model to all the workers as step 1 communication (*Figure 10.3*).

To sum up, after looping over the four communication steps (*Figures 10.3-10.6*), we can enable the workers to share their knowledge (local model weights) without sharing their local input data.

Next, we will illustrate a case study on the TensorFlow Federated platform.

Case study: TensorFlow Federated

Here, we will discuss **TensorFlow Federated** (**TFF**) as a case study.

TFF is based on TensorFlow and enables TensorFlow to conduct federated learning.

In order to use it, you need to first install it as follows:

```
# installation
#first step
pip3 install tensorflow
# GPU support
pip3 install tensorflow-gpu
#second step
pip3 install tensorflow_federated
```

After installing, you can make a function call by importing the libraries you installed as follows:

```
# To use TensorFlow Federated
# First Step
import tensorflow as tf
# Second Step
import tensorflow_federated as tff
```

After that, you can start writing code for federated learning using TensorFlow.

In a nutshell, TFF mainly has two-layer APIs as follows:

- Federated Learning APIs
- Federated Core APIs

These two layers are shown as the top two layers in the following figure:

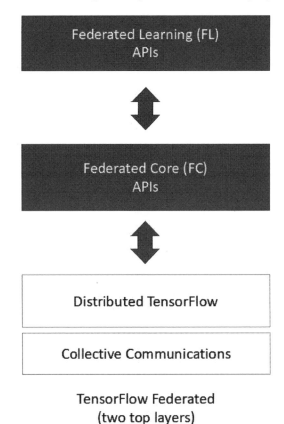

Figure 10.7 – Two-layer (top two) structure of TFF

As shown in the preceding figure, TFF consists of two layers: the Federated Learning APIs layer and the Federated Core APIs layer.

The Federated Learning APIs layer is responsible for providing user-level APIs that help users to use it easily.

The Federated Core APIs layer serves as an intermediate layer between Federated Learning APIs and other TensorFlow APIs. At a high level, the Federated Core APIs layer translates the Federated Learning APIs to more detailed and complicated TensorFlow APIs.

For more information, you can refer to the TFF official website here: https://www.tensorflow.org/federated.

Next, we will discuss another new concept, called TinyML.

Running edge devices with TinyML

After the model is trained using the federated learning approach that we have discussed so far, we want to deploy the trained model and conduct efficient model inference/serving. This leads to the concept of TinyML.

The deploy hardware of edge devices usually has a lot of constraints. Let's look at these constraints and how we can tackle them:

- **Limited battery power**: This means that our deployment should be very efficient and cannot consume a lot of battery power.

- **Unstable connection to the server**: This means that we need to guarantee that the model is still usable if the device cannot connect to the server.

- **High latency for communication**: This means that if some emergency happens, the model deployed on the device can handle it without coordinating with the central server.

- **Data locality**: This means that we need to keep each device's local data private and never allow the local data to communicate with other devices.

The preceding four challenges are the main requirements of TinyML. Next, we will discuss how TensorFlow Lite handles all the preceding challenges one by one.

Case study: TensorFlow Lite

Given the four challenges defined in TinyML, the TensorFlow team implemented a specific platform for TinyML called **TensorFlow Lite**.

Now let's talk about how TensorFlow Lite handles each of the TinyML challenges one by one here.

First, to reduce the total power consumption, TensorFlow Lite can run the model without maintaining the following metadata:

- Layer dependency
- Computation graph
- Holding intermediate results

Second, to avoid the unstable connection issue, TensorFlow Lite removes all the unnecessary communication between the server and devices. Once the model is deployed on the device, normally no specific communication is needed between the central server and the deployed devices.

Third, to reduce the high latency for communication, TensorFlow Lite enables faster (real-time) model inference by doing the following:

- Reducing the code footprint
- Directly feeding the data into the model as the data does not require unpacking

Finally, to guarantee the data locality, TensorFlow Lite mainly targets the model inference stage. This means that the local data on each device only passes into the local model on the device for inference. There is no communication at all between any of the devices that we deploy the models to.

For more information, you can refer to TensorFlow Lite's official website here: `https://www.tensorflow.org/lite`.

Summary

In this chapter, we mainly discussed a new method of distributed machine learning, called federated learning. The key concept of federated learning is that it enables collaborative model training without sharing each worker's local data. Thus, federated learning makes it possible for data privacy applications such as multiple banks to collaboratively train a model for fraud detection, for example.

After reading this chapter, you should understand how federated learning works via sharing knowledge without sharing real data. You should also understand how to use the TFF platform for federated learning. In addition, you should understand the concept of TinyML and its requirements. Finally, you should have learned how TensorFlow Lite satisfies all the requirements of TinyML.

In the next chapter, we will learn about elastic model training and serving.

11
Elastic Model Training and Serving

The one big challenge in distributed DNN training is determining how many GPUs or accelerators to use for a single training or inference job. If we assign too many GPUs to a single job, it may waste computational resources. If we assign too few GPUs to a particular job, it may lead to an insanely long training time. In addition, this choice of the number of GPUs is also highly relevant to choosing the corresponding hyperparameters (such as batch size and learning rate) during the whole DNN training session. How to choose the appropriate quantity of accelerators is the main topic we cover in this chapter. In addition, we will also explore hyperparameter tuning accordingly.

Before we discuss anything further, we want to list our assumptions, as follows:

- We assume you have an infinite number of GPUs or TPUs or other accelerators to use for DNN training and inference.

- We assume you use homogeneous GPUs or other kinds of accelerators.

- We assume you're adjusting the number of GPUs to use during the training period of a single job.

- We assume you have lower bandwidth for cross-machine communication and higher bandwidth for intra-machine communication.

- We do not allow job preemption or job interrupts.

- Each of our training/serving jobs uses the whole GPU exclusively, which means there is no resource sharing among different jobs.

- We assume you have adjusted the batch size and learning rate in the middle of your training session.

- We assume you have full bandwidth for inter-machine and intra-machine communication.

- We assume you can guarantee that the batch size you have selected will not cause an out-of-memory error.

- We assume you have selected the batch size that will lead to model convergence.

In this chapter, we will mainly cover the topic of system efficiency in distributed DNN training and inference. More specifically, we will discuss adaptive resource allocation for distributed machine learning workloads.

First, we will discuss elastic model training with the case study of the **Pullox** system. Second, we will provide implementation instructions for elastic model training in a public cloud, such as AWS. Third, we will discuss the concept of elastic model serving. Fourth, we will talk more about serverless computing, which is a good use case for elastic model training and inference.

After going through this chapter, you will understand what adaptive model training is. You will also have learned how to adjust the number of GPUs to use for a single job. You will understand how to adjust the learning rate and batch size when the number of GPUs changes. For model inference, you will learn how to conduct elastic model serving, and how to use serverless computing for elastic model training and serving.

In a nutshell, you will learn about the following topics:

- Adaptive model training

- Implementing adaptive model training in the cloud

- Elasticity in model inference

- Serverless

Now, we will first discuss adaptive model training. Before diving into the details, we'll list the technical requirements in the following section.

Technical requirements

We assume you're using PyTorch and its relevant platforms for your implementation platform. The main library dependencies for our code are as follows:

- `torchtext>=0.5.0`
- `portpicker>=1.3.1`
- `pytest-aiohttp>=0.3.0`
- `pip>19.0`
- `numpy>=1.19.0`
- `python>=3.7`
- `ubuntu>=16.04`
- `cuda>=11.0`
- `torchvision>=0.10.0`
- NVIDIA driver >=450.119.03

It is mandatory to have the preceding libraries preinstalled with the correct versions.

Introducing adaptive model training

Here, we'll discuss elastic model training. In the following sections, we may use *adaptive* and *elastic* interchangeably, as they have similar meanings.

Adaptive model training is where we can change the number of GPUs during the training process. To better illustrate what we mean by changing the number of GPUs during the training process, we'll first describe how traditional distributed DNN training works with a fixed number of GPUs.

Traditional data parallel training

In normal distributed data parallel training, we assign our training job to a fixed number of GPUs, as shown in the following figure:

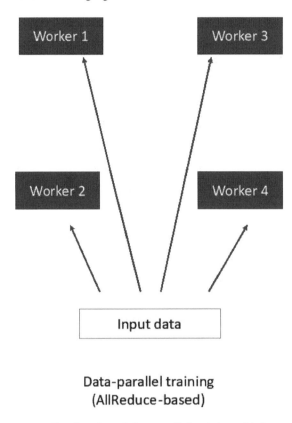

Data-parallel training
(AllReduce-based)

Figure 11.1 – AllReduce-based data parallel training with four workers

As shown in the preceding figure, one data parallel training paradigm is **AllReduce**-based. In this setting, we fix the number of workers to four. Therefore, for each training iteration, we do the following:

1. Feed four batches of input data into four different GPUs.
2. Each GPU conducts local model training.
3. All the GPUs use the AllReduce function to conduct model synchronization.
4. Loop over the preceding three steps.

However, as you can see here, the number of GPUs is fixed before we conduct model training and the number of GPUs in use remains the same for the whole model training session.

For parameter server-based data parallel training, we also need to pre-assign a fixed number of GPUs before conducting model training. The parameter server-based data-parallel training looks as follows:

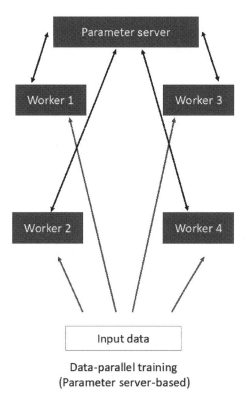

Data-parallel training
(Parameter server-based)

Figure 11.2 – Parameter server-based data parallel training with four GPUs

As shown in the preceding figure, in parameter server-based data parallel training, we first need to fix the number of GPUs to use. Here, we chose four GPUs. Then, we conduct the following steps:

1. Feed different input data batches into different GPUs.
2. Each GPU conducts local model training.
3. All the GPUs communicate their local gradients with the parameter server.
4. The parameter server aggregates all the local gradients from all the GPU workers and updates the model.
5. The parameter server broadcasts the updated model weights to all the GPU workers simultaneously.
6. Loop over the preceding five steps.

Similar to AllReduce-based data parallel training, in parameter server-based data parallel training, we also need to fix the number of GPUs we use before conducting any training job. For each training job, the number of GPUs in use is also fixed during the whole model training session.

Adaptive model training in data parallelism

In contrast, adaptive model training may change the number of GPUs in use during the DNN training process.

Let's simplify this process into two stages. We call the first half of the training iteration the **early stage**. We call the second half of the training iteration the **late stage**. There are two widely believed rules for distributed DNN training, as follows:

- We should use a large learning rate and small batch size in the early stage of the training job.

- We should use a small learning rate and large batch size in the late stage of the training job.

Therefore, we can get to the following conclusion:

- In the first half of the training iteration, since we need a small batch size, we can use fewer GPUs.

- In the second half of the training iteration, since we need a large batch size, we should use more GPUs.

Therefore, by adjusting the number of GPUs to use in the middle of the DNN training session, we can use the GPUs more efficiently.

Adaptive model training (AllReduce-based)

To better illustrate the preceding idea, let's first take AllReduce-based data parallel training as an example.

It contains two stages. The first stage is the early stage, where we should use fewer GPUs (that is, workers). We depict the early-stage training process in *Figure 11.3*:

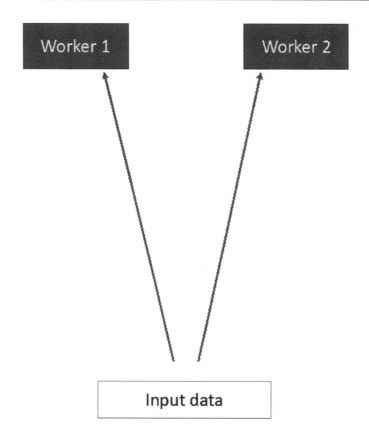

**Adaptive data-parallel training
(AllReduce-based, early stage)**

Figure 11.3 – Adaptive data parallel training at the early stage (AllReduce-based)

As shown in *Figure 11.3*, during the early stage of our adaptive DNN training, instead of using four GPUs, as done in *Figure 11.1*, here we just use two GPUs. Since at the early stage we usually only need a small batch for training, we can save computational cost here.

During the late stage (second stage) of the DNN training, since we choose a smaller learning rate, we need a much larger batch size for in-parallel training. Therefore, we should use more GPUs concurrently.

The following figure depicts the late stage of AllReduce-based adaptive training:

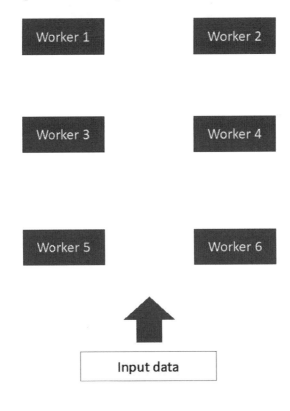

**Adaptive data-parallel training
(AllReduce-based, late stage)**

Figure 11.4 – Adaptive data parallel training at a late stage (AllReduce-based)

As shown in *Figure 11.4*, since we need a large batch size during the late stage of the DNN training, we may use more GPUs at this late stage. Here, we choose to use six GPUs at the late stage for large-batch data parallel training.

Note that compared to the fixed GPU solution in *Figure 11.1*, our adaptive training solution uses the same amount of computational resources. Since in the early stage we use two GPUs (instead of the four in *Figure 11.1*), we can use four plus the two we saved in the early stage together and use these six for the late-stage, larger-batch training.

Adaptive model training (parameter server-based)

Now, let's look at the parameter server-based adaptive model training.

Similarly, here we also split the whole training session into two parts:

- Early stage (first half of the training iterations)
- Late stage (second half of the training iterations)

The following figure depicts the early-stage adaptive training in AllReduce-based data parallelism:

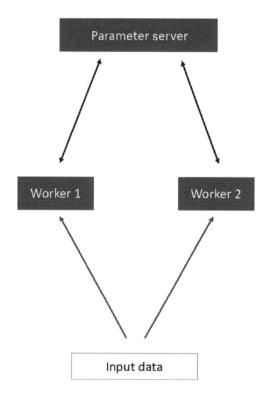

Data-parallel training
(Parameter server-based, early stage)

Figure 11.5 – Adaptive training in the parameter server paradigm (early stage)

As shown in the preceding figure, we also choose to use a small batch during the early stage of the training process. Thus, we use fewer workers at the early training stage. As shown in *Figure 11.5*, we choose to use only two workers here.

For the late stage of parameter server-based DNN training, we also choose to use more GPUs. The details are shown in the following figure:

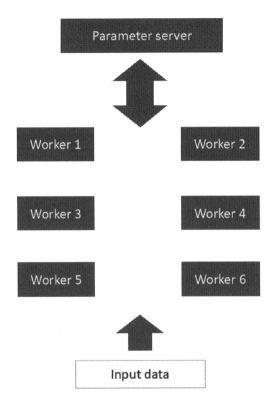

Data-parallel training
(Parameter server-based, late stage)

Figure 11.6 – Adaptive training in the parameter server paradigm (late stage)

As shown in the preceding figure, we need a larger batch for late-stage DNN training. Thus, we choose to use six GPUs (that is, workers) in this case.

In a nutshell, by using adaptive data parallel training, we can increase the model's convergence rate. Thus, we can speed up the end-to-end DNN training process. At the same time, we use similar computational resources as the fixed number of GPU solutions.

Next, we will discuss how traditional model-parallel training works and how we can incorporate adaptive model training into model parallelism.

Traditional model-parallel model training paradigm

Let's first look at the traditional model-parallel training paradigm. In traditional model-parallel training, we need to fix the number of GPUs in use first. The normal model-parallel training process is depicted in the following figure:

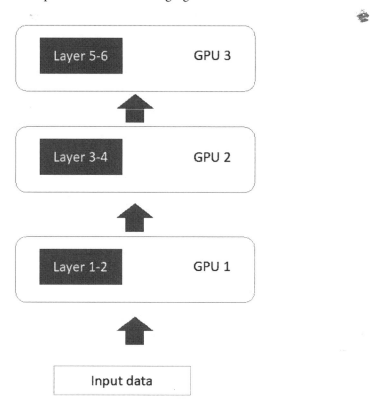

Model-parallel Training

Figure 11.7 – Model-parallel training of a six-layer DNN model

As shown in the preceding figure, in traditional model-parallel training, we need to fix the number of GPUs to use first. Here, we choose to use three GPUs together. Since we have a six-layer DNN model, we split the model as follows:

- **Layer 1** and **Layer 2** on **GPU 1**
- **Layer 3** and **Layer 4** on **GPU 2**
- **Layer 5** and **Layer 6** on **GPU 3**

During the whole training session, we use this fixed number of GPUs (three GPUs in *Figure 11.7*) and we cannot adjust the quantity of GPUs in use in the middle of the training session.

Adaptive model training in model parallelism

Now, let's discuss how adaptive model-parallel training works here.

Similar to the adaptive data parallel training, here we also simplify the training process into two stages: the early stage and late stage.

During the early stage, we monitor the training process of each layer. The detail is shown in the following figure:

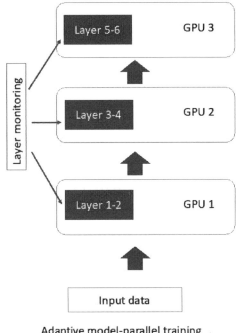

Adaptive model-parallel training
(early stage)

Figure 11.8 – Adaptive model-parallel training at the early stage

As shown in the preceding figure, we have a layer-monitoring module during the adaptive model training stage. It monitors whether a layer is converged or not. The criteria for determining convergence is very simple:

- If the gradients are almost zero, it means this layer is converged.
- Otherwise, the layer is not converged.

After the early stage finishes and before we jump into late-stage training, we need to determine the layers that are already converged. Thus, we can free these layers. The detailed implementation is shown in the following figure:

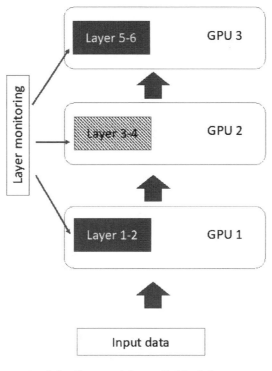

Figure 11.9 – Freezing layer 3-4 on GPU 2 at the end of early-stage training

As shown in the preceding figure, after the early-stage training finishes, we first determine the layers that are already converged. Here, we assume layer 3 and layer 4 on **GPU 2** are converged. Therefore, we freeze these two layers. Then, we try to incorporate adaptive model-parallel training to use fewer GPUs in the late-stage training.

It works as follows:

1. We freeze the layers that are converged, which means for a later-on training session, these layers won't generate activations.

2. We merge these frozen layers with other GPUs, so we can empty the GPUs that initially held these frozen layers.

3. Then, we conduct late-stage DNN training with fewer GPUs in use.

Figure 11.9 shows *Step 1*. *Step 2* is shown in the following figure:

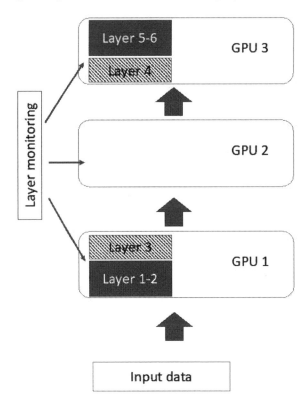

Figure 11.10 – Adaptive model training before the late stage starts

As shown in the preceding figure, by splitting the frozen layers on **GPU 2** to **GPU 1** and **GPU 3**, we now empty the model partition on **GPU 2**. Thus, we can remove **GPU 2** from our training job and use fewer GPUs for late-stage training.

The late-stage adaptive model-parallel training is shown in the following figure:

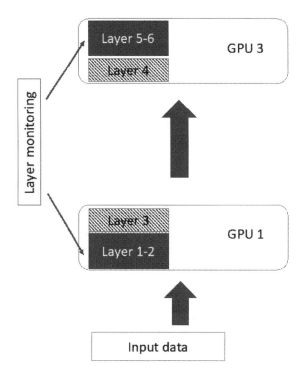

Adaptive model-parallel training
(late stage)

Figure 11.11 – Adaptive model-parallel training at the late stage

As shown in the preceding figure, by removing **GPU 2** from our training job, we can now use fewer GPUs at the late stage of the training job.

Next, we will briefly discuss the implementation of adaptive model training.

Implementing adaptive model training in the cloud

Here, we discuss how to implement adaptive model training using PyTorch on AWS.

First, we need to install the corresponding Python packages:

```
# installation
pip3 -m pip install adaptdl
```

Once the package is successfully installed, we can use it for adaptive and distributed DNN training, as follows:

```
#import package
import adaptdl
# Initialize process group
adaptdl.torch.init_process_group("MPI")
# Wrap model to adaptdl version
model = adaptdl.torch.AdaptiveDataParallel(model, optimizer)
# Wrap data loader to adaptdl version
dataloader = adaptdl.torch.AdaptiveDataLoader(dataset, batch_
size = 128)
# Start adaptive DNN training
remaining_epoch = 200
epoch = 0

for epoch in adaptdl.torch.remaining_epochs_until(remaining_
epochs)
...
train(model)
...
```

Basically, we need to wrap both the model and input data with the adaptdl version. Then, we can conduct the normal DNN training and adaptdl will handle how to conduct the adaptive DNN training under the hood.

If you want to learn more details about how to use adaptdl, more information can be found on its official GitHub page here: https://github.com/petuum/adaptdl.

Next, we will discuss elastic model inference.

Elasticity in model inference

After the model is fully trained, we can use it for parallel model inference. However, traditional model inference also needs to predefine how many workers/GPUs to use for a serving job.

Here, we discuss a simple solution of elastic model serving. It works as follows:

- If the number of concurrent inference inputs is higher, we use more GPUs for this model-serving job.

- If the number of concurrent inference inputs is lower, we shrink down the number of GPUs we use.

For example, right now we have received four concurrent model-serving queries, as shown in the following figure:

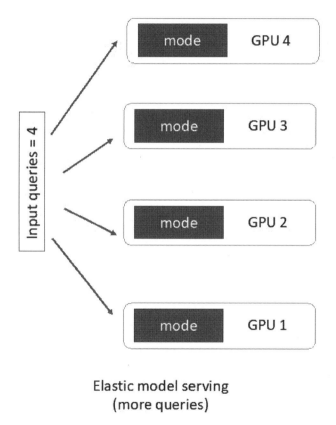

**Elastic model serving
(more queries)**

Figure 11.12 – Elastic model serving with more queries

As shown in the preceding figure, if we have more queries, we can use more GPUs to do concurrent model serving in order to reduce the model-serving latency.

On the contrary, if we have fewer queries, for example, we only have one query, as shown in the following figure, we can shrink down the number of GPUs in use:

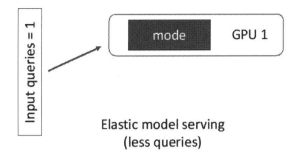

Figure 11.13 – Elastic model serving with fewer queries

As shown in the preceding figure, in the case we have only one query, we can reduce the number of GPUs in use to just one, which reduces the computation cost without increasing the model-serving latency.

Next, we will discuss how to use adaptive model training and elastic model serving in the cloud environment.

Serverless

Note that AWS offers a serverless computing environment, which is a perfect fit for this adaptive scheme we have discussed so far.

Basically, if we want to use more GPUs, we can query for more concurrent computation resources from AWS Lambda. Similarly, if we want to use fewer GPUs, we can query fewer concurrent computation resources from AWS Lambda.

Summary

In this chapter, we mainly discussed adaptive model training and elastic model serving. At a high level, we can adjust the number of workers/GPUs to use in the middle of our model training or serving session.

After reading this chapter, you should understand how adaptive DNN training works in both data parallelism and model parallelism. You should also be able to implement adaptive model training using the `adaptdl` library. You should know how elastic model serving works and how to use an AWS serverless computing environment for computation resource requests.

In the next chapter, we will discuss more advanced techniques for further DNN training and serving speed-ups.

12
Advanced Techniques for Further Speed-Ups

So far, we have discussed all the mainstream distributed **Deep Neural Network** (**DNN**) model training and inference methodologies. Here, we want to illustrate some advanced techniques that can be used along with all the previous techniques we have.

In this chapter, we will mainly cover advanced techniques that can be applied generally to DNN training and serving. More specifically, we will discuss general performance debugging approaches, such as kernel event monitoring, job multiplexing, and heterogeneous model training.

Before we discuss anything further, we will list the assumptions we have for this chapter, as follows:

- By default, we will use homogenous GPUs or other accelerators for model training and serving.

- For heterogeneous model training and inference, we will use heterogeneous hardware accelerators for the same training/serving job.

- We have Windows Server so that we can directly use NVIDIA performance debugging tools.

- We will use GPUs or any other hardware accelerators exclusively, which means the hardware is used by a single job only.

- We have high communication bandwidth among all GPUs within a single machine.

- We have low bandwidth for GPU communication across different machines.

- The network between the GPUs is also used by a single training or serving job exclusively.

- If we move the training/serving job among GPUs, we assume the overhead for data movement is just a single shot.

- For model training and serving in a heterogeneous environment, we assume it is easy to achieve load balancing between different accelerators.

First, we will illustrate how to use the performance debugging tools from NVIDIA. Second, we will talk about how to conduct job migration and job multiplexing. Third, we will discuss model training in a heterogeneous environment, which means we use different kinds of hardware accelerators for a single DNN training job.

After going through this chapter, you will understand how to use NVIDIA's **Nsight** system to conduct performance debugging and analytics. You will also acquire the knowledge of how to do job multiplexing and migration in order to further improve the system efficiency. Last but not least, you will learn how to carry out model training in a heterogeneous environment.

In a nutshell, you will understand the following topics after going through this chapter:

- Debugging and performance analytics
- Job migration and multiplexing
- Model training in a heterogeneous environment

First, we will discuss how to use the performance debugging tools provided by NVIDIA. But before diving into the details, we'll list the technical requirements for this chapter.

Technical requirements

You should be using PyTorch and its relevant platforms for your implementation platform. The main library dependencies for our code are as follows:

- NVIDIA Nsight Graphics >= 2021.5.1
- NVIDIA drivers >=450.119.03
- `pip` >19.0
- `numpy` >=1.19.0
- `python` >=3.7
- `ubuntu` >=16.04
- `cuda` >=11.0
- `torchvision` >=0.10.0

It is mandatory to have the preceding libraries pre-installed with the correct versions.

Debugging and performance analytics

In this section, we will discuss the NVIDIA Nsight performance debugging tool. You will learn how to use this tool for GPU performance debugging.

Before using the tool, you should first download and install it. The web page for downloading is here: `https://developer.nvidia.com/nsight-systems`.

After downloading and successfully installing the tool, we will learn how to use it. The following is the command line for collecting NVIDIA profiling information using Nsight Systems:

```
# Profiling
nsys [global-option]
# or
nsys [command-switch] [application]
```

After collecting the profiling information, the system will log all the activities on the GPUs for performance analysis later on.

If your system only has one GPU, you will get the performance information as shown in the following figure:

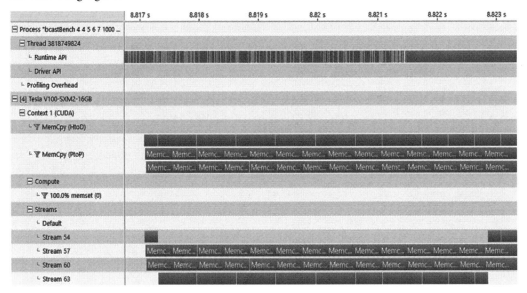

Figure 12.1 – Single GPU profiling details using the NVIDIA Nsight profiler

As shown in the preceding figure, we can see two devices' logs, one from the CPU and the other from the GPU.

More specifically, the top bars for **Thread 3818749824** are all the instructions running on the CPU side. All the bottom bars are CUDA instructions running on **Tesla V100-SXM2-16GB**, which is on the GPU side.

If your system has more than one GPU, all the device logs will be shown on the same graph. The following figure shows the results of two GPUs plus one CPU profiling:

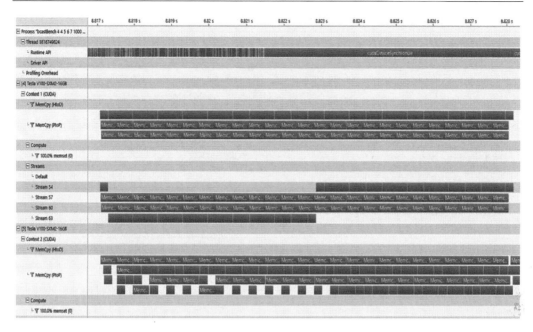

Figure 12.2 – Multi-GPU profiling results from the NVIDIA debugging tool

As shown in the preceding figure, besides the CPU instructions (that is, **Thread 3818749824**) as the top bars, we have two GPUs' log results.

The first GPU is [**4**] **Tesla V100-SXM2-16GB** and the second GPU is [**5**] **Tesla V100-SXM2-16GB**.

Here, we conduct some GPU data transfer, which is shown as **Memc** boxes in *Figure 12.2*. **Memc** in *Figure 12.2* stands for mem_copy, which basically means copying one GPU's data to another GPU's on-device memory.

So far, we have had a brief overview of what these profiling results look like. Next, we will discuss the general concepts within these profiling results.

General concepts in the profiling results

Since we are focusing on the GPU performance analysis, we will ignore the CPU instruction details here. For the following sections, we will mainly focus on the GPU log results.

Basically, the NVIDIA profiler will log two main things: **computation** and **communication**. A simple example of this is as follows:

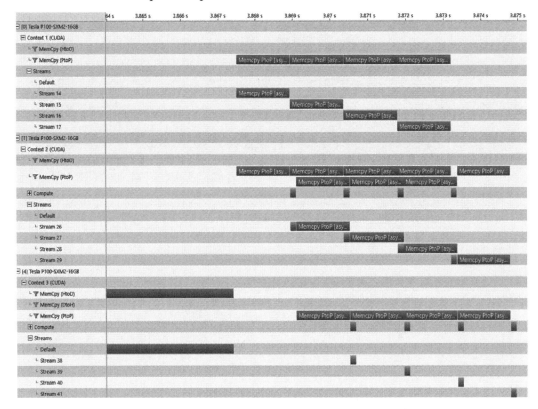

Figure 12.3 – Simple profiling example including both computation and communication

As shown in the preceding figure, we use GPUs 0, 1, and 2, which are denoted as **[0] Tesla P100-SXM2-16GB**, **[1] Tesla P100-SXM2-16GB**, and **[4] Tesla P100-SXM2-16GB**, separately. They are denoted as such because on the V100 GPU, the yellow bars are too short to be recognized (which means the operations take less time than P100 GPUs).

On the computation side, all the computation events will be shown under the category of **Compute** in *Figure 12.3*. Also, each GPU has a single **Compute** row for monitoring its local computation kernels.

As shown in *Figure 12.3*, there is no **Compute** row for GPU 0 (that is, **[0] Tesla P100-SXM2-16GB**), which means that no computation happens on GPU 0 while this job is running.

For GPU 1 (that is, **[1] Tesla-P100-SXM2-16GB**), we can see that the compute row exists. It launches four computation kernels, as follows:

- The first is at timestamp **3.869 s**.

- The second is between timestamps **3.87 s** and **3.871 s**.

- The third is at timestamp **3.872 s**.

- The fourth is at timestamp **3.873 s**.

On the communication side, we can look at the rows under the **Context** category of each GPU.

For example, on GPU 0 (that is, **[0] Tesla-P100-SXM2-16GB**) in *Figure 12.3*, we conducted some **MemCpy (PtoP)** communication operations from **3.867 s** to **3.874 s**, which is shown as boxes under **Context 1 (CUDA)** on GPU 0. Similarly, **MemCpy** also happens on other GPUs, such as GPU 1 (that is, **[1] Tesla-P100-SXM2-16GB**) and GPU 4 (that is, **[4] Tesla-P100-SXM2-16GB**).

Next, we will discuss each category in detail. First, we will discuss the communication analysis among GPUs. Second, we will talk about the computations on each GPU.

Communication results analysis

Here, we discuss the communication patterns in detail. A simple example that covers all the communication patterns is shown in the following figure:

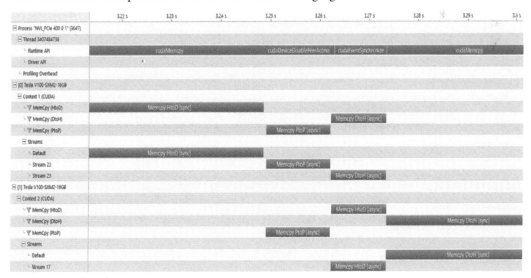

Figure 12.4 – Simple example that covers all communication patterns among GPUs

As shown in the preceding figure, we mainly have three types of data communication among GPUs:

- **MemCpy (HtoD)**: This means we conduct memory copy from **Host (H)** to **Device (D)**. Host means the CPU and device refers to the current GPU.

- **MemCpy (DtoH)**: This means we conduct memory copy from **D** to **H**. It means we transfer data from the GPU to the CPU.

- **MemCpy (PtoP)**: This means we conduct memory copy from **Peer to Peer (PtoP)**. Here, peer means GPU. Thus, PtoP means GPU-to-GPU direct communication without involving the CPU.

Let's take *Figure 12.4* as an example. GPU 0 (**[0] Tesla V100-SXM2-16GB**) has the following communication operations:

1. It first conducts **MemCpy (HtoD)** (*sync*), which means it receives data from the CPU side.

2. After that, it conducts **MemCpy (PtoP)** (*async*), which means it sends data to another GPU (GPU 1 in this case).

3. After that, it conducts **MemCpy (DtoH)** (*sync*), which means it sends data to the CPU side.

Similarly, the data communication pattern also happens on GPU 1.

Next, we will discuss computation results analysis.

Computation results analysis

Here, we will discuss the second main part of performance analysis, that is, **computation kernel launching**.

Let's first look at an example involving computation that is simpler than *Figure 12.3*. A simpler version of CUDA/compute kernel launching is as follows:

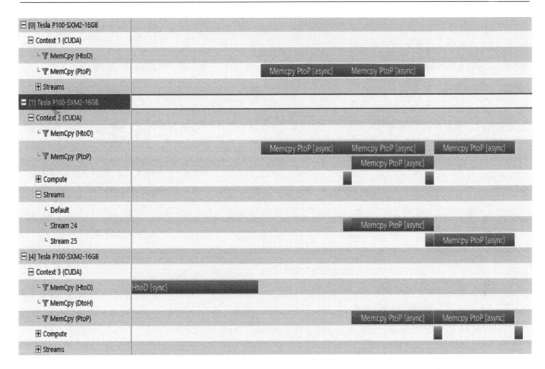

Figure 12.5 – A GPU job involving two computation kernels on GPU 1 and GPU 4

As shown in the preceding figure, in this simplified version, we have two computation kernels launching on GPU 1 ([1] **Tesla-P100-SXM2-16GB**) and GPU 4 ([4] **Tesla-P100-SXM2-16GB**) separately, which are shown in the **Compute** row.

In addition, by looking at the **Streams** category, we can see that two compute kernels on each GPU are launched on different streams.

For example, on GPU 1, the first compute kernel is launched on **Stream 24**, and the second kernel is launched on **Stream 25**.

Here, each stream on the GPU can be regarded as a thread on the CPU side. The reason for launching multiple streams concurrently is to use the in-parallel computation resource as much as possible.

Now, let's click on the + symbol in front of **Compute** on **GPU 1**. We get the following:

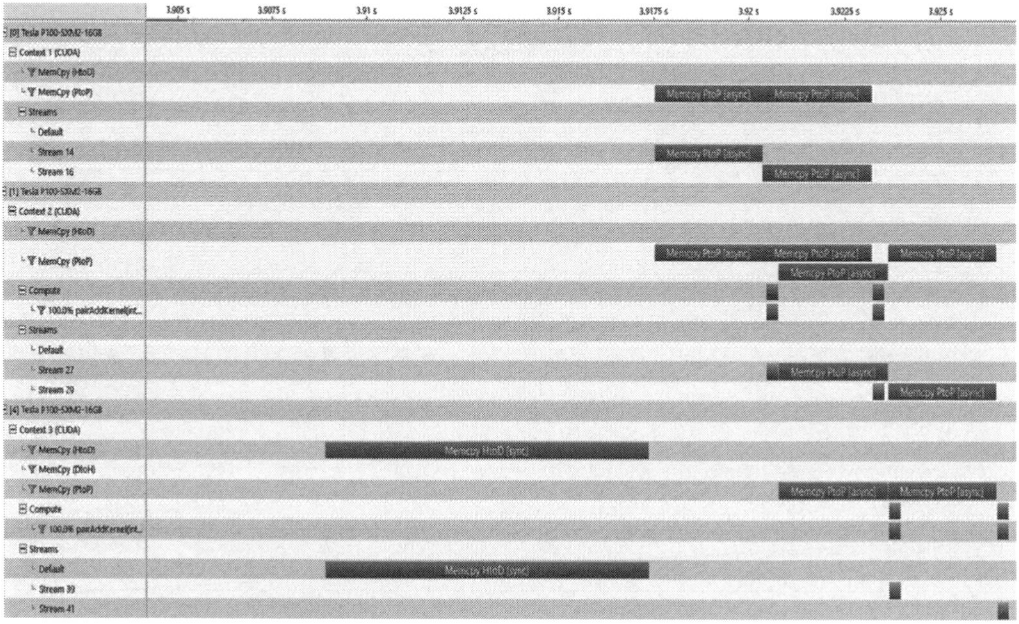

Figure 12.6 – Expanding the Compute row to see the kernel information

As shown in the preceding figure, once we expand the **Compute** category on **GPU 1** (**[1] Tesla P100-SXM2-16GB**), it shows the CUDA/computation kernel name right below the **Compute** row.

Here, the CUDA kernel we are making a function call to is named **pairAddKernel**. Basically, it tries to add two large arrays together on the GPU.

If you want to know more details about the kernel information, you can click on each kernel box inside the **Compute** row. It will show you the detailed kernel information, as shown in the following figure:

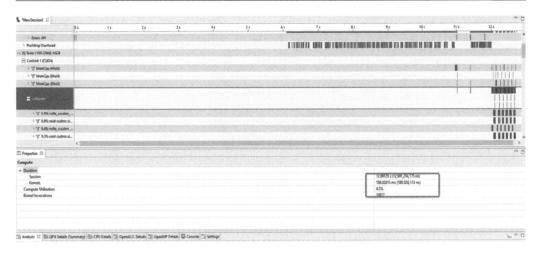

Figure 12.7 – CUDA kernel details are shown at the bottom of the table

As shown in the preceding figure, once we click on any computation kernel inside the **Compute** row, the bottom table shows the details of the computation kernel. Here, it shows the following properties of the computation kernel:

- Compute utilization (4.5%)

- Kernel session (launching time) (12.99123 s)

- Kernel duration (588.02615 ns)

So far, we have discussed how to use the NVIDIA performance profiler to debug and analyze GPU performance on both the communication and computation sides.

For more details, you may refer to NVIDIA's Nsight official user manual page here: `https://docs.nvidia.com/nsight-systems/2020.3/profiling/index.html`.

Next, we will discuss the topic of job migration and multiplexing.

Job migration and multiplexing

Here, we'll discuss DNN training job migration and multiplexing. We will first discuss the motivation and operations for job migration.

Job migration

The first thing we will discuss here is why we need job migration. A simple example to understand this operation is shown in the following figure:

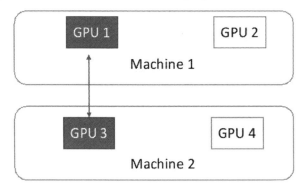

Figure 12.8 – A single training job is assigned to GPU 1 on Machine 1 and GPU 3 on Machine 2

As shown in the preceding figure, in a cloud environment, there is the case that a single DNN training job can be split across multiple machines. As per one of our assumptions at the beginning of this chapter, cross-machine communication bandwidth is low. Therefore, if we conduct frequent model synchronization between **GPU 1** and **GPU 3**, the network communication latency is very high. Thus, the system utilization is very low.

Due to the low system efficiency, we want to move GPUs working on the same job into the minimum number of machines. Merging GPUs into the minimum number of machines is what we call **job migration**.

In the case of *Figure 12.8*, we want two GPUs on one machine rather than one GPU on one machine and the other GPU on the other machine. Thus, we conduct job migration by moving all the data and training job operations from **GPU 3** to **GPU 2**, as shown in the following figure:

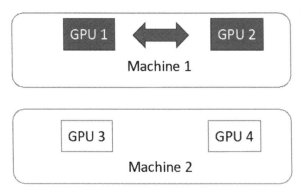

Figure 12.9 – Job migration to Machine 1

As shown in the preceding figure, after the job migration, we move the training job to two GPUs (**GPU 1** and **GPU 2**) located on the same machine (**Machine 1**). Since the GPU communication bandwidth within one machine is much higher than cross-machine, we improve system efficiency by doing this job migration.

Job multiplexing

Job multiplexing is a general concept to further improve system efficiency. Basically, there are cases where a single job may not fully utilize a GPU's computation power and on-device memory. Thus, we can pack multiple jobs onto the same GPU to improve system efficiency significantly. Packing multiple jobs onto the same GPU is what we called **job multiplexing**.

A simple example can be when we have two identical training jobs. Each one can utilize 50% of the GPU computation power and 50% of the GPU on-device memory. Thus, instead of training one job at a time, we can pack these two jobs together onto the same GPU and train the two jobs concurrently.

Next, we will discuss how to conduct model training in a heterogeneous environment.

Model training in a heterogeneous environment

This is not a very general case. The motivation for heterogeneous DNN model training is that we may have some legacy hardware accelerators. For example, a company may have used NVIDIA K80 GPUs 10 years ago. Now the company purchases new GPUs such as NVIDIA V100. However, the older K80 GPUs are still usable and the company wants to use all the legacy hardware.

One key challenge of doing heterogeneous DNN model training is load balancing among different hardware.

Let's assume the computation power of each K80 is half of the V100. To achieve good load balancing, if we are doing data parallel training, we should assign N as the mini-batch size on K80 and $2*N$ as the mini-batch size on V100. If we are doing model-parallel training, we should assign 1/3 layers on K80 and 2/3 layers on V100.

Note that the preceding example for heterogeneous DNN training is simplified. In reality, it is much harder to achieve decent load balancing between different hardware accelerators.

By doing good load balancing between different types of GPUs, we can now conduct a single DNN model training job in a heterogeneous environment.

Summary

In this chapter, we discussed how to conduct performance debugging using NVIDIA profiling tools. We also introduced job migration and job multiplexing schemes to further improve hardware utilization. We also covered the topic of heterogeneous model training using different hardware simultaneously.

After reading this chapter, you should understand how to use NVIDIA Nsight for GPU performance debugging. You should also now know how to conduct job multiplexing and job migration during DNN model training or serving. Finally, you should also have acquired basic knowledge of how to conduct single-job training using different hardware concurrently.

Now, we have completed all the chapters for this book. You should understand the key concepts in distributed machine learning, such as data parallel training and serving, model-parallel training and serving, hybrid data and model parallelism, and several advanced techniques for further speed-ups.

Index

Packt.com

Subscribe to our online digital library for full access to over 7,000 books and videos, as well as industry leading tools to help you plan your personal development and advance your career. For more information, please visit our website.

Why subscribe?

- Spend less time learning and more time coding with practical eBooks and Videos from over 4,000 industry professionals

- Improve your learning with Skill Plans built especially for you

- Get a free eBook or video every month

- Fully searchable for easy access to vital information

- Copy and paste, print, and bookmark content

Did you know that Packt offers eBook versions of every book published, with PDF and ePub files available? You can upgrade to the eBook version at packt.com and as a print book customer, you are entitled to a discount on the eBook copy. Get in touch with us at customercare@packtpub.com for more details.

At www.packt.com, you can also read a collection of free technical articles, sign up for a range of free newsletters, and receive exclusive discounts and offers on Packt books and eBooks.

Other Books You May Enjoy

If you enjoyed this book, you may be interested in these other books by Packt:

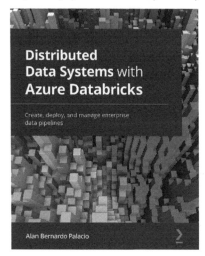

Distributed Data Systems with Azure Databricks

Alan Bernardo Palacio

ISBN: 9781838647216

- Create ETLs for big data in Azure Databricks

- Train, manage, and deploy machine learning and deep learning models

- Integrate Databricks with Azure Data Factory for extract, transform, load (ETL) pipeline creation

- Discover how to use Horovod for distributed deep learning

- Find out how to use Delta Engine to query and process data from Delta Lake

- Understand how to use Data Factory in combination with Databricks

- Use Structured Streaming in a production-like environment

Machine Learning with the Elastic Stack - Second Edition

Rich Collier, Camilla Montonen, Bahaaldine Azarmi

ISBN: 9781801070034

- Find out how to enable the ML commercial feature in the Elastic Stack
- Understand how Elastic machine learning is used to detect different types of anomalies and make predictions
- Apply effective anomaly detection to IT operations, security analytics, and other use cases
- Utilize the results of Elastic ML in custom views, dashboards, and proactive alerting
- Train and deploy supervised machine learning models for real-time inference
- Discover various tips and tricks to get the most out of Elastic machine learning

Packt is searching for authors like you

If you're interested in becoming an author for Packt, please visit `authors.packtpub.com` and apply today. We have worked with thousands of developers and tech professionals, just like you, to help them share their insight with the global tech community. You can make a general application, apply for a specific hot topic that we are recruiting an author for, or submit your own idea.

Share Your Thoughts

Now you've finished *Distributed Machine Learning with Python*, we'd love to hear your thoughts! Scan the QR code below to go straight to the Amazon review page for this book and share your feedback or leave a review on the site that you purchased it from.

https://packt.link/r/1-801-81569-0

Your review is important to us and the tech community and will help us make sure we're delivering excellent quality content.

Made in the USA
Coppell, TX
25 July 2023

19598470R00157